REVOLUTIONARY LOVE

Revolutionary Love

FESTO KIVENGERE
with Dorothy Smoker

CHRISTIAN LITERATURE CRUSADE
ALRESFORD
and
KINGSWAY PUBLICATIONS
EASTBOURNE

Kingsway ISBN 0 86065 333 1
CLC ISBN 0 90028 457 5

Front cover photo: Susan Griggs Agency, London

Printed in Great Britain for
KINGSWAY PUBLICATIONS LTD
Lottbridge Drove, Eastbourne, E. Sussex BN23 6NT by
Cox & Wyman Ltd, Reading

CONTENTS

by Roy Hession
(Author of *The Calvary Road*)

I am delighted to welcome and recommend this book by my friend and brother, Festo Kivengere. We have already teamed up in various parts of the world, ministering the message of grace together. I owe much to the message of the East Africa revival, from which Festo comes, and am only too glad to be identified with him.

There is more in this book than meets the eye. It purports to be Festo's personal testimony together with the message he delights to give. But in doing this, he gives the discerning reader new and beautiful insights into the East Africa revival, about which there has been a growing interest among Christians in the West. There has, of course, always been an intense interest among the people of God worldwide in the working of God in revival; and as this movement of revival has continued for more than fifty years, beginning in about 1930 and continuing unabated right up to the present day, it has rightly commanded their attention, accompanied as it is with so much of deep challenge. But in actual fact, how few have understood its inner lessons and applied them to their lives! This book should help here, because it is not a reporter's account from the sidelines but rather a personal testimony from the middle of the "scrum," or as the Americans would say, "scrimmage," referring to their form of football. It is one thing to speak of spectacular events which are sometimes associated with revival, but it is far more important to know what Jesus is doing in the middle of that scrum. And we shall not know unless someone emerges from it, muddied and gory, to tell us what he has experienced there. Then we can ask ourselves the all-important question, Is Jesus doing the same in us?

Well, Festo has come out of that revival scrimmage. He came under conviction of sin and into liberty in Jesus through it; he

3

has lived out his new life in Jesus in the fellowship of the revival brethren there, and what he has to give to others he has learned along with them. So he can really tell what is going on in the heart of revival. But you have got to look for it. Note the fellowship through which and into which he was saved—beginning with the man who brought back eight cows to the hard pagan chief, Festo's uncle, with the confession that he had stolen them and he was bringing them back because he had been saved by Jesus. "He has given me peace," he said, "and He has told me to bring them." Does the average conversion associated with our fellowship have this effect? Would that it did. Note, too, all the other lessons he learned with his new brothers and the further steps he took. If we embark with them on this sort of path of openness and brokenness, receiving in a deeper way the grace of God for sinners, we would have to confess, "We have not passed this way before."

Festo does not set out to tell us in any direct way about the East Africa revival or of revival generally. Indeed, the word hardly occurs. He relates his experience with Jesus and applies his message, simply telling it as it is. But if you see the implications of it all and begin to respond to the Lord, you will find that God is already beginning revival in your own experience.

For myself, I am so glad that the team of missionaries and African leaders who came to England in the years around 1947 in order to share with us what they had been learning in revival did not confuse the issue by telling us stories of signs and wonders and spectacular happenings, but limited themselves to giving their testimony of God's dealings with them and the simple message of the grace of God and the power of the blood of Christ on which it was all based. As a busy but defeated evangelist, I was stopped in my tracks. What they said about themselves in their pre-revival days was exactly my condition then. I had to face the One who "is light and in whom is no darkness at all," and I found that as I said *yes* to what His light revealed and as I continued to do so, "the blood of Jesus Christ, His Son, cleanses me from all sin" and brings me into liberty.

This book may well have the same effect on many of its readers. May it be so.

Roy Hession

Revolutionary Love

The title of this little book may sound strange to many, both Christians and non-Christians. This strangeness may be the result of the unusual combination of what to most of us seems to involve a "parting of the ways," a movement in opposite directions!

Revolution—understood usually as a negative, violent, destructive and fanatical turning upside down of the good and established things of life—leaves lives shattered, empty and miserable.

Love—commonly understood as a positive, harmless, stabilizing thing, a satisfaction with things as they are—is the custodian and preserver of what one possesses from the past and the protector of what makes life enjoyable in the present. Love, in this sense, is the direct opposite of the disturbing elements embodied in revolution, which threatens what the present possesses. Such love will fight with all its established weapons against the "tomorrows" of any new vision of life— be it spiritual renewal, social progress, political or economic change.

But *true love* is a revolutionary experience. Love between two persons always changes them. Love of art revolutionizes the artist. Love of nation revolutionizes the citizen. And far above any of these revolutionary human loves is the love of Christ, causing the most radical revolutionary experience in human life.

A certain notorious religious fanatic, one who did not hesitate to torture and execute those he considered dangerous to his established religious traditions and the security they offered—Saul, by name—met Jesus on the road to Damascus. Here two revolutionaries met head on: Saul using *revolutionary hate,* and Jesus using *revolutionary love.*

Jesus' love penetrated the entire person of Saul that day. Wave after wave of Christ's revolutionary love went through him, warming, sensitizing, melting, enlightening, transposing all his values and transforming the foundations of all his systems of understanding. The end result of that event is poignantly put in Paul's own words in 2 Corinthians 5:14-17: ''The love of Christ leaves me no option (having revolutionized my whole life—mind, thought, word and action!). . . . For when anyone is in Christ, he/she is a new (revolutionized) person altogether.''[1] This is not an evolution or reformation but a newly created person!

It is Christ's revolutionary love that Africa desperately needs to bring radically new relationships between clans, tribes, nations, races, political parties and ideologies. It alone can cure economic exploitation, rampant corruption, unjust laws and hostility between religious denominations. My own entire set of values was exchanged for new ones when Christ met me forty years ago, and that transvaluation still continues at a deeper level today.

On the cross of Calvary—there for all to see and be exposed to—God in Christ launched His revolutionary love as the only ''Operation Hope'' for His chronically fragmented but beloved human race.

I pray that through the shared messages of this book—by the power of the Holy Spirit—you will open up to this revolutionary love of Christ and experience a radical transformation of the foundations of your entire system of life. May He do His work in and through you.

Festo Kivengere

[1] *Personal paraphrase*

CHAPTER 1

Love and the Unlovable

What a shock I had when I reached home!

My eagerness to arrive had made the dust and bumps of the long journey seem nothing. So I was definitely unprepared for the situation I found as the old lorry I was riding in pulled into Rukungiri, my home town in Western Uganda.

It was 1939. I was nineteen and coming home with the ink barely dry on my teacher's certificate. I had been given my first teaching position in the very boys' school I had attended. That pleased me. At least it would be a start, and I would have money in my pocket.

The first ugly surprise came when the truck rounded the marketplace. A crowd had gathered around some people who were singing church songs right out in public! Imagine hearing this floating over the fruit and vegetables: "Down at the cross where my Saviour died...." To me that was sheer fanaticism.

The headmaster was waiting for me in town, which was gratifying. Some of my relatives were there also. My favorite niece threw her arms around me and cried, "Uncle Festo, welcome home! I love Jesus now. Do you, too?"

I grunted something and changed the subject. As an agnostic, I was quite offended.

As the days passed, the situation proved worse than I had thought. People, both young and old, were caught up in a sort of religious frenzy, doing ridiculous things. Many of them had been good churchgoers for years, but this was something quite new.

They would talk about Jesus in all sorts of places, and you never knew where they might burst out in song. It was infectious, spreading like a disease.

We "enlightened" young people were angry. We maintained that church people ought to confine their singing to church buildings and not spread it out onto public roads and into marketplaces. Women going to draw water were praising Jesus—how unsuitable!

You might walk up to the home of a friend and find a circle of neighbors sitting in the courtyard singing and sharing. When you tried to slip away unnoticed, they would call to you. A decent person didn't know where to hide.

My mother's brother, the senior chief of our district, was appropriately tough against such things. He was a good chief, selected by the British government as the most progressive of the sons of the former king, my grandfather. It was his policy to be a strong supporter of both the church and the schools brought in by British missionaries. When my widowed mother had sent me to him, I had lived in his big compound and had gone to school nearby. He never tolerated any tardiness at prayers or absence from church services.

Now, however, my uncle said, "This new kind of religion is dangerous. It invades your privacy. You have nothing left."

There were other unsettling aspects of it for the chief to consider. Those women who were "saved" no longer covered their faces before men, and they spoke out in public as if they were set free from the ancient traditions. Even worse, the customary distinction between our tribe and the local Iru tribe was ignored by these extremists. They actually ate meals together, breaking the food taboos of hundreds of years! And in many other ways they ignored the feelings of the revered ancestors, thereby bringing the danger of calamity upon the whole land. Church people had never done these things before. They had been as careful as anyone else not to offend the spirits of the ancestors.

My uncle, the chief, felt he had to take action, and so he told his retainers that they could beat up the ones who spoke

10

of being "saved." Some of them were thrashed severely.

Beating didn't change them, and sometimes the results were the reverse of what my uncle intended. A court official would beat up a man because he talked about Jesus publicly, but when the beater went home he couldn't sleep. By morning he was weeping and went off to join the fanatics. Exasperated, my uncle changed his order: "Don't beat them. That is dangerous. You might become like them."

One day he arrested twenty of the committed Christians on some pretext and sent them off under guard to the British head-quarters for trial. Uganda was under British rule at that time. The prisoners and guards had to walk for two days to get there. On the way, the prisoners were singing and telling the officers what Jesus had done for them.

The first night, when they camped and sat around the fire, one of the guards turned to Jesus. Later, when the District Commissioner released the prisoners, they went off singing and gathered quite a parade of followers along the way home. The converted guard went to report to my uncle and included his testimony in the report. You can imagine the problem my uncle had. No one was safe.

I was having difficulties of my own. The school where I taught was a mission school, and I was expected to attend the local church. That wouldn't have been hard except that near-ly everyone who was asked to speak or preach was one of the fanatics. What they said was always dangerously personal. We were constantly bombarded with talk about the cross. Those preachers always dragged in disturbing subjects even when they started from perfectly safe stories, such as Adam and Eve. I smiled to think how those two had jumped over God's fence in order to broaden their opportunities. But then there was always talk about "the voice of the Lord God, who was walking in the garden in the cool of the day." *Why* was God supposed to be grieving and wanting to bring them back inside the fence? And *why* did that make the cross inevitable? What was the connection? It was oppressive.

They preached about Cain, and I could sympathize with him.

11

There was an independent fellow for you! I thought, "Who wants to be his brother's keeper anyway?" His loneliness and ostracism I blamed on social injustice and resented the conclusions the preachers came to.

One person to whom I could relate easily was the younger son, in the New Testament story, who said something like this:

"Father, I am bored stiff! I am sick and tired of this home. Every day is a repetition. I want to be free and find myself. I want to be authentically human. Dad, I want to live! Just give me what belongs to me—what I should get if you were dead—and I will go."

I could daydream about how he enjoyed spending money endlessly in the city for pleasures with his friends. But I preferred to slip out of the church when they began to talk about the money and friends being gone and about the father who waited for him.

Actually I knew what it was to be an angry young man who was tired and lonely and finding life increasingly unmanageable and confusing. I was running as far away as I could from this Jesus they talked about, determined never to surrender to Him or to anyone except myself.

I was the kind of agnostic who is not interested in trying to prove whether there is a God or not. Once I had gone along with these "saved" people, when I was a youngster in boarding school at Kabale. I had made some confessions when others were doing that too, and it felt good for a while. But when they said God wanted me to do something hard, I revolted. After that I ignored God and eventually said He was not there. I wished to be free. When you know the truth and rebel against it, you become strangely hard.

Sitting with my uncle, the chief, I could thoroughly appreciate his dilemma. However, neither of us could say that these people were total frauds. Take the matter of cattle.

We were a cattle people. To my tribe, cows were what made life worth living. By the time I was three, I knew the name of every one of my father's 120 cows, bulls and calves. Some men I knew thought more of their cattle than of their children.

12

So there were many things that happened that were incredible.

For instance, one day the chief was holding court and his elders were listening to his wisdom when a man arrived who was well known to be a pagan and wealthy in cattle. His servants had eight fine cows they were driving along. All the elders turned to look at them appreciatively.

The cattle baron greeted everyone, and then said, "Your Honor, I have come for a purpose."

The chief answered, "Fine. What are these cows for?"

"Sir, they are yours. I have brought them back to you."

"What do you mean, they are mine?"

"Well, sir, when I was looking after your cattle, I stole four of them when I told you we had been raided. These four are now eight. I have brought them to you."

"Who discovered this theft?"

"Jesus did, sir. He has given me peace and told me to bring them."

There was dead silence and no laughter. It was quite a shock. My uncle could see that this man was rejoicing, and all knew that what he had done was impossible for a man of our tribe.

"You can put me in prison, sir, or have me beaten. I deserve it. But I am at peace and a free man for the first time."

"Humph!" said my uncle. "If God has done that for you, who am I to put you in prison? Leave the cattle and go home."

A day or two later, when I saw my uncle, I said, "I hear you got eight good cows free."

"Yes, it's true."

"You must be happy."

"Forget it! Since that man came, I can't sleep. If I wanted the peace he has, I would have to return a hundred cows!" For the time being, however, he went right on resisting, and so did I. Nevertheless, we admitted that some power we had not seen before was at work in our tribe, and we tried to think up some good explanations.

I was hating God because the awareness of Him embarrassed me continually. I was running away from "churchianity," from the Bible and from clergy. I wanted to escape this business

13

of being "holy." I simply wanted to be my own manager.

My life was turning round itself like a spinning top. A top has a big head and a thin base, so it can't stand up unless it is spinning round and round. If it slows down, it topples over. It depends on spinning to keep going.

My spinning cycle was work-play-eat-drink-sleep-work-play-eat-drink, and so on, round and round. The more humdrum it became, the speedier I got. I thought that the faster I went, the livelier life would be. But I was finding out that a directionless life is difficult to live.

Though I pushed them back, my sins were dark against me and threatening. Guilt pursued me like a hunting dog after its prey. I was a man ill at ease—young, but fragmented inside, a victim of perpetual civil war.

Of course, I was running headlong into self-destruction. At the age of nineteen I considered ending my life. It was not because I didn't have health or work or party friends; it was because the things I did lacked meaning. There was a hollowness inside and life seemed lonely and undependable. There was a haunting sense of uncertainty. Perhaps what happened then was because I had come to the end of hope and was looking at suicide. In a way, I felt I was drowning. It was rather like my first attempt to swim.

Near the first boarding school I went to was a deep river. Most of the boys knew how to swim but I never learned. I watched them as they jumped into the river, both short and tall boys, shouting and having great fun.

I grumbled, "Some of these kids are not even as tall as I am, and they are enjoying the river. They can keep their heads above water, so why can't I? I have arms like theirs, and legs. Why not try?" So I took off my shirt and jumped into the pool.

I don't have to tell you what happened next. I went down like a stone. My arms were thrashing and my feet wouldn't respond. Again I went down, came up, and swallowed a lot of water doing it.

Boys being boys, those watching on the shore were clapping and laughing and having a good time seeing this new fellow sink. They did nothing while I was struggling, but watched until my strength was gone. Then a big boy jumped in and came swimming toward me. By the time he reached me, I was utterly unable to help myself. Now I was rescuable. The boy reached out, grabbed me, and swam to the shore.

Perhaps the One from whom I was running so fast saw that I was now rescuable, and He had arranged an encounter for me on a certain day. He also had some people praying.

My sister, who was twelve years old, and my niece, fourteen, were staying with me and attending the girls' school. They were concerned that I was a "lost" teacher, and I could sometimes hear them praying for me. I didn't make it easy for them either, because I was careless and full of myself.

One Sunday morning I went to church and the service was full of "fire." After the first song, young people were giving their testimonies and people were being converted even before the preacher began to preach. As usual, I sat at the back near the door just in case things got hotter as the service went on.

Then, who should ask permission to speak but my niece! She said, "I want you to praise God. The devil has been making me afraid of telling you what the Lord has done for us. On Friday night the Lord assured us that our prayers for Festo are answered. And Festo is sitting in the corner right there, and we know that he is going to come back to the Lord today."

So I got up and went outside, absolutely in a rage. I spent that day drinking hard at my uncle's place, planning to come back and make things difficult for this girl who was foolish enough to take the liberty of speaking about me in public like that.

Late that afternoon I was cycling home, somewhat wobbly, when I saw a good friend of mine riding his bicycle toward me on the dusty road, with a look on his face as if he were flying. He was a teacher, like me, and I knew very well that he did not ordinarily have a glow on his face. I was surprised.

My friend pulled up beside me and said, breathlessly, "Festo! Three hours ago Jesus became a living reality to me. I know my sins are forgiven!"

He had never before spoken with any enthusiasm about Jesus. Then with complete sincerity, he said, "Please, I want you to forgive me, friend, . . ." and he named three specific things for which he wanted forgiveness, related to some questionable things we had done together. "I am sorry, Festo. I will no longer live like that. Jesus has given me something much better. So long!"

Off he went, whistling exuberantly, leaving me with my mouth open there on the road. If only he had stayed to let me argue . . . but he did not.

His joy overwhelmed me. His words, and the way he said them, shook me to the core. I felt like a shadow, having seen in my friend the reality I had missed. I cycled home utterly miserable and empty.

When I reached my room, I knelt by my bed, struggling for words to the One in whom I no longer believed. Finally I cried, "God! If You happen to be there, as my friend says, I am miserable. If You can do anything for me, then please do it now. If I'm not too far gone . . . HELP!"

Then what happened in that room! Heaven opened, and in front of me was Jesus. He was there real and crucified for me. His broken body was hanging on the cross, and suddenly I knew that it was my badness that did this to the King of Life. It shook me. In tears, I thought I was going to Hell. If He had said, "Go!" I would not have complained. Somehow I thought that would be His duty, as all the wretchedness of my life came out.

But then I saw His eyes of infinite love which were looking into mine. Could it be He who was clearly saying, "This is how much I love you, Festo!"

I shook my head, because I knew that couldn't be possible, and said, "No, I am Your enemy. I am rebellious. I have been hating Your people. *How can You love me like that?*"

Even today, I do not know the answer to that question. There is no reason in me for His love.

But that day I discovered myself clasped in the Father's arms. I was tattered and afraid, just like the younger son who went

16

into the far country and then came to the end of himself. But *why* should the Father, who is holy, come running to hold *me* to His heart? I was dirty and desperate and had said and done much against Him.

That love was wholly unexpected, but it filled my room, and I was convinced. He is the only One who loves the unlovable and embraces the unembraceable. In spite of what I was, I knew I was accepted, was a son of the Father, and that whatever Jesus did on the cross, it was for me.

Ever since that day, the cross has been central in my thinking, and the Lord Jesus my Enabler for living near to it. I want to share some of what He is doing for me and what He will do for you by His Calvary love.

CHAPTER 2

Loved into Joy

That afternoon when I encountered Jesus Christ, I was completely surprised by what I now know was the inrushing of the Holy Spirit. He came and put the risen King on His throne in my heart. He flooded me with the love of God and with irrepressible joy. I began jumping and shouting there in my little room.

There was no one about and I needed to tell someone, so I rushed out onto the road and hailed the first person I met, shouting, ''Jesus has come my way! I'm forgiven!''

The person was a Christian woman, a church member, but perhaps she thought I was mocking, as usual, for she went off wagging her head.

I had to find someone else, so I ran to the church. God's people were still there and had been there ever since the morning service, because one after another had been finding Jesus that day. This was a common occurrence in Uganda in those days.

When I burst in, I excitedly told them my news and they took me into their arms, singing and rejoicing. Some laughed and some wept for joy. One after another embraced me with comforting words. Others did a kind of happy dance around me. One big man put me on his shoulder and walked around with me, not realizing that he was acting like the shepherd who said, ''Rejoice with me, for I have found my sheep which was lost.''[1] My little sister and my niece were there and I loved them. They had been expecting me.

One beautiful thing was that I was welcomed equally by

the saints of the various tribes, and I now felt entirely different toward the people of other tribes than I ever had. I knew we were all one, and it was beautiful. The cross that rescued them had rescued me and the tribal barrier was gone.

When we all sat down, my tears were flowing fast, and so one of the brothers read from the New Testament the story of the sinful woman weeping at Jesus' feet.[2]

I could picture that street woman after meeting with Jesus in the house of Simon the Pharisee. She must have rushed out of the house and begun telling everyone she met about her forgiveness. No doubt she found herself in the arms of Mary Magdalene and the other forgiven ones. I can hear her telling them all about it.

"I was miserable and lonely for so long and kept hearing about Jesus of Nazareth. So today when I saw Him going into the house of this Pharisee, I just followed Him in. I know Simon is judgmental and hard, but I *had* to see Jesus and nothing could keep me out.

"Jesus was reclining at table . . . " is perhaps the way she told them, "and they hadn't even been decent enough to wash His feet. I know, because I was holding them, and my tears came like a flood. I couldn't help weeping, because the burden was so great. I've hated myself and the life I've lived, and Jesus was so totally different from any man I ever knew before.

"When He turned and looked at me, I knew He understood me. His eyes were full of forgiving love that filled me with light and warmth. My heart began to vibrate because something wonderful was happening. No one accepts me, but He accepted me! I felt cleansed, covered, and put together.

"My tears kept coming and I was kissing His feet, wiping them with my hair. I poured my perfumed oil on them. You can imagine how cold Simon looked—his eyes were like daggers. He was muttering ugly things to his friends against the Master. But Jesus was willing to take the blame and be misunderstood for me. Imagine that! The very words He said were: 'Your sins are forgiven. Your faith has saved you. Go in peace.' So now I am free and He is *my Lord* forever."

20

I had those same feelings and tried to speak them. All around me that Sunday evening my new brothers and sisters were listening to me and encouraging me and reading me the Scriptures. Each word was fresh and exciting, as though I had never heard it before. Over and over we sang the chorus:

Yes, I'm washed
In the blood,
In the soul-cleansing blood
Of the Lamb!

The Lamb! That was it. Suddenly the Old Testament account I had read in school fell into place. I could see an Israelite who knew he was a lawbreaker trudging toward the Tent of Meeting in the Sinai Desert with a lamb in his arms. I knew about white, spotless lambs because I had played with them when I herded my father's calves and sheep.

This man with the condemning heart would not have dared to go into the presence of God if he had not had with him this lamb, the provision God had ordained for the guilty. I could see him give it to the priest and then carefully lay his hand on its head.[3]

He watches as the lamb's blood is spilled, knowing that God is graciously reckoning the lamb's death instead of his own. When it is done, the priest pronounces the man forgiven, and peace comes to his heart.

"I lay my sins on Jesus, the spotless Lamb of God," sang my new brothers and sisters. Yes, God's Lamb was Jesus. What a costly sacrifice! How could the Father be willing to let His beloved Son leave Heaven to become the Lamb for my sin offering? But He did. And Jesus, hanging on the cross, was looking into my eyes, saying, "This death of Mine is reckoned as your death. Now you may have peace."

The new peace from Him was confirmed to me by the brothers and sisters who fully accepted me as one of the forgiven. They did for me the work of the priest at the door of the Tabernacle who assured the man with the lamb that now he was right with God.

One after another of God's family told me how Jesus had

met him or her, and I was amazed at the variety of encounters, but always it was Love running to the rescue, to fill emptiness, to embrace loneliness, to wash away filth.

Later in the evening, some of the group accompanied me back to my house and warmed it with singing. Someone brought in some food, but better yet was the spiritual nourishment of the conversation as they told me what Jesus was doing for them.

They stayed on, and I think it was while they were praying that my mind drifted away and doubt invaded me when my eyes were closed.

I seemed to be standing in a courtroom before a severe judge and I was afraid. From one side and another there were voices accusing me. My own conscience was the prosecutor, presenting a pile of claims. They were like IOUs I had to pay. Witnesses were gazing at me reproachfully—I knew their faces.

"You were not honest here," droned the prosecutor. I looked down.

"You acted in a mean way."

"Mmm."

"You failed morally."

I had nowhere to look. On and on it went.

When you buy, you have to pay. When you sin, you have to suffer. That is what my heart told me. The Law told me so, too. I pretended I had forgotten some of the charges, but I hadn't. And even the things in my life I was proud of didn't help me out.

I stood bankrupt in the court of Law. I knew what it was to be insolvent, without a cent in my moral bank account. Condemned.

Then, oh, the wonder!

God Himself stepped into the courtroom. Steadily, firmly, He picked up all the things which had wrecked my humanity, all the nasty experiences of my sinful nature, all my accumulated guilt, all the accusations against me, and put them on the shoulders of His God-Man. Jesus voluntarily chose to take on Himself the responsibility for all I owed.

22

My heart was crying out words something like those of the hymn writer:

> Nothing in my hand I bring,
> Simply to Thy cross I cling;
> Naked, come to Thee for dress;
> Helpless, look to Thee for grace;
> Foul, I to the fountain fly;
> Wash me, Saviour, or I die![4]

All at once release came again—and joy.

When I looked up, I saw that my new family sitting around the room were still praying and praising God. I was able to share with them about the courtroom and how I was acquitted.

They nodded and said, "Yes, we have stood there, too. His love drew you to see yourself as He sees you and to stand under the righteous condemnation of Heaven. Now you know what Jesus willingly took on Himself—it was all for you."

"His gift to you," they said, "is the strength to do what He asks: just repent and believe Him. The forgiveness is already complete, and so you felt it instantly without waiting. 'There is therefore now no *condemnation* for those who are in Christ Jesus.' "[5]

Wonderful! Do you know what it is to have "no condemnation" singing like a bell in your heart? Can you accept it with *both* hands? With *both* feet? Let me explain.

The first time I was in London I was in a subway train called "The Underground." When the train stopped and I stepped out onto the platform with my suitcases, I discovered that the "WAY OUT" sign pointed only to a moving staircase, an escalator. I had never seen one before and it scared me.

For a while I watched other people get onto it and go up. Finally my need to get out began to overcome my fear of the moving stairway. Slowly, holding my bags tightly, I put one foot on the escalator.

Of course, being an automatic machine, it didn't wait for me to get more courage. It took that one leg up, and I fell backwards! Two English people directly behind me saw that I was a stranger in trouble, and they put on me what I call

23

"gentle pressure." Firmly, but without embarrassing me, they got me onto the staircase with both feet and both suitcases.

What a change! Suddenly, and gratefully, there was nothing to worry about, not even a load to carry. The stair took me and my cases right up to the top. Accepting forgiveness is stepping on with *both* feet to what God in Christ has already done for you. I did that, and God's family saw it.

The brothers stayed at my house all night, quietly singing and praying.

No one urged me, or suggested it, but because of an inner nudging, I brought out my cigarettes and threw them away. We sang, "Glory to His Name!"

They kept on praising God and I gathered up other things from boxes that I wanted to get rid of in my new life. It was a kind of housecleaning, accompanied by singing.

Finally they insisted that I go to bed. I did and I slept like a baby—an unusual thing for me at that time.

In the morning we all went to our work.

In the evening they came back and stayed with me another night, singing, praying and reading the Bible, for which I now had a tremendous appetite.

"Why do you do this?" I asked one of the brothers. "Why do you love me so much?"

"Because Jesus first loved me," he answered.

For three days it was like Heaven in my house. This is the way they broke the loneliness of one who had been far away. That is how Calvary love came to me in its first spring flood from Jesus Christ and from His brothers and sisters who loved me into His joyous Kingdom.

- - - - - -

1 Luke 15:6, *KJV*.
2 Luke 7:36-50.
3 Leviticus 4:32-35.
4 "Rock of Ages," Augustus Toplady.
5 Romans 8:1, *RSV*.

CHAPTER 3

Love Reconciles

In our community, after Christians were liberated by the power of the risen Lord, people of all sorts were shaken by contact with them.

Take, for instance, a Muslim shopkeeper. One day a customer came into his shop and said, "Here, these 200 shillings are yours. I cheated you out of this money and you didn't find out." He explained how it happened.

"Well! Why do you bring it now?"

"Jesus has changed my life and has told me to pay my debt to you. I felt poor with your 200 shillings in my pocket, but I am a rich man now that you have them. Please forgive me."

In those days that was a lot of money, and so when the man left, the shopkeeper's mouth was gaping.

Some British officials were jarred. At times there were so many people waiting outside to return or pay things that the district commissioner complained that it was hard to get his work done.

A man would say, "I have evaded my taxes for ten years; here is a cow to pay them."

Another would say, "Here, sir, please take this shovel which I stole from the government when I worked on the road crew."

The officer would ask, "Why did you bring it back?"

"I was arrested, sir."

"Who did that?"

"Jesus did."

Some British colonial officers were educated agnostics, but they learned some practical theology from humble people.

25

When Jesus took hold of me, these believers in whose fellowship I found myself said, "Be careful to *obey* the Lord. Do quickly whatever He tells you to do."

Gradually I realized that I had a lot of things to make right. The Monday morning after I met Jesus, before starting to teach my class in the boys' school, I asked them to forgive me for treating them as mere cases to receive instruction. I told them that Jesus had turned me around and opened my eyes to see them as my precious brothers.

Most of the boys were glad. All were surprised.

After school and on weekends, Jesus sent me to the town and through the fields to people I had cheated, slandered, or hurt, to ask forgiveness. Paying debts came easy. When the risen Christ takes His throne in the heart, no poverty is there, because He is King, rich in mercy, grace and fullness. The Holy Spirit floods the heart and liberates the whole personality.

My uncle, the chief, resented what had happened to me because I had been his stalwart ally.

He crossed my name out of the tribal book as dead.

Then one night his wife was converted in their bedroom. There was no preacher there. The Holy Spirit simply penetrated the room. The woman woke up crying like a baby and began asking my uncle's forgiveness for a great many things. He shouted, "This thing is invading even the bedroom at night. There is no privacy left!"

Our women used to put veils over their faces to hide their beauty. Now the chief's wife put off the veil and began to speak publicly. Everbody expected her to collapse and faint, but she told the new things that Jesus had done for her. She was talked about everywhere, and my uncle was sick with anger. Whatever had happened to tradition and the ancient culture?

After fifteen years of battle, in the year 1956, my uncle surrendered to Jesus Christ. He returned thousands of shillings to people he had falsely fined. People he had oppressed he summoned and asked to forgive him. He emptied his bank account and gave back many head of cattle. All knew that the chief had changed, and his enemies became his friends.

At his funeral, there was a great gathering. Christians were singing "Hallelujah" and speaking the praises of the Saviour. The occasion became a resurrection as well as a burial because a number of people came to the Lord, including his own elder brother, another uncle of mine who had been a staunch pagan.

One day soon after I met the Lord I felt God was saying to me, "Go and be reconciled with your step-father." He was not a Christian and things had been bad between us for years. So I went to his home with a feeling of fear. What would he do to me?

He was sitting outside his home. He looked at me coldly. I mumbled and blurted out something about the hatred I had had for him being gone and that I loved him now.

"I knew you hated me," he observed, studying me.

"You knew only a little. I came to tell you the whole story and to say that it is all over. Please forgive me."

An hour later he rose and put his arms around me, and we stood there for a while. I was overcome. I never expected such a reaction, but love is a language which anyone can understand. The barrier was gone and we became friends; our homes are open to each other.

Nothing short of Jesus' poured-out love on the cross could have made possible the mending of that estrangement. Not even the tribal ceremony of the "Karabo" (Atonement) could have done it.

In our tribe the "Karabo" was a ritual that was supposed to end hatred and revenge. It was done after there had been a murder, usually an accidental one when people were drunk. It was in order to prevent more killing, for otherwise revenge would have been taken on all the members of the murderer's clan.

When the family of the killer acknowledged the culprit's guilt and sought reconciliation, then all the elders of the tribe were called together in solemn assembly under the sacred oak in the presence of the king.

With all the witnesses around him, the priest slaughtered

a perfect cow or sheep at the junction of two main paths. Both the offender and one of the offended, in slow motion, and savoring the meaning of it, laid down their weapons. Together they came to the sacrifice and plunged their hands into the blood. Then they soberly shook hands, each using both hands.

An audible sigh of relief could be heard around the circle. Dancing and celebration followed. Now there could be no more thought of avenging the dead. The heads of all the clans had witnessed that the guilt was taken care of and the hatred was supposed to be dissolved. The customary laws of hospitality were restored and normal brotherly loyalty in the tribe observed. Outwardly this worked, but it takes the far costlier sacrifice of the bleeding love of God's Son to heal inward resentments.

I experienced the effectiveness of that healing on a weekend soon after. The Holy Spirit had reminded me that I hated a white man—a missionary. He lived fifty miles away, so I thought I need not do anything. But the Spirit said, ''Take your bicycle on the weekend and go to see this man. Now that you are liberated, he is your brother.''

''My *brother*? An Englishman?'' I nearly fell over.

''Yes, your brother. You have hated your brother.''

''What shall I do when I see him? You know him, Lord.''

''Yes, I know him. Tell him that you love him.''

That fifty miles to Kabale had never seemed so hard. The rivers seemed much wider than usual and the escarpment steeper than I had ever seen it. Approaching the house, I was tired and frightened and hoped he was not at home.

He was there, and suddenly I was standing in his proper English living room telling him what Christ had done for me, that I was free, and saw him now as my brother.

''I'm sorry,'' I said. ''For the past five years I have hated you and talked against you. I must have made your life terribly difficult. Please forgive me.''

English though he was, there were tears in his eyes and we put our arms around each other. When I left, I was no longer his enemy but his beloved brother. What a change!

On the way home, my bicycle flew as if it had a motor on

it. My heart was beating fast, my world was different, and in that house there was no longer a lonely "European" but a brother—a true brother to this day. Many times since then I have proved that the cross is the end of race prejudice, and of separating walls of all kinds.

Zacchaeus, the little publican, came into that same kind of joy after he had been at a distance from society.[1] In Jesus there was a hand outstretched to restore him to the humanity he had lost. The warmth of God's Son penetrated that guilty heart, releasing him from his prison.

I can see him standing there, his face relaxed, with the corroding forces of selfishness removed. His values had changed and he couldn't help saying, "Master, if I have cheated or defrauded anyone, I will restore it fourfold!"

The scribes must have fidgeted. They had never heard anything like that before.

The following day in his office, "Zack," as I call him, was explaining to a man about his taxes: "You paid sixty, but ten of that I stole. I am returning fourfold, so here, take this forty."

"Wha-at! What happened?"

"Jesus of Nazareth came home with me, and I no longer feel the same. I have discovered myself and you too!"

When that man told his news, there must have been a line-up outside Zack's office. So enmities died and walls were removed in the light of the love of God...who gave the gift of humanity and knows how to restore it.

I don't believe that those first wonderful days were the last time in Zack's life that he knew the fresh joy of restoration into the love of God and the love of his fellows. If his experience was anything like mine and others, he heard again and again, in the years that followed, that quiet Inner Voice[2] that spoke of what had gone wrong to bring in tension or a barrier, and he took the quick way back into fellowship—the way of the cross.

- - - - - -

[1] Luke 19:1-9.
[2] John 16:8.

CHAPTER 4

Love's Quick Way

When I was a boy, I loved sliding down a long, steep slope on a thick clump of banana leaves. At the top you sit on the banana leaves, which are slippery, and push off. . .and down you go. A-ah! It is beautiful to go down. No effort at all. The problem is in getting back up again. The way is steep and slow, and the banana stalk is heavy to carry.

I have found in life that it is very easy to slide downhill spiritually. I simply choose to have my own way instead of God's, or to react with selfishness, and down I go. But how do I come up again?

As a teenager I slid away from God, and when I saw that the way back was hard, I gave it up, walked away, said the game wasn't fun, and eventually doubted the existence of the top of the hill.

People have told me that there are slow, hard ways to climb back up the hill of broken relationships, but the brethren who nurtured *me* taught me early that the quick way back was by the cross of Christ and by agreeing with the Holy Spirit. It is costly and not always easy, but it is instantaneous.

When, after my encounter with the Lord, I first realized that some distance had again come between me and Him, I wanted to forget it. I thought that if I ignored it, it would go away. I kept on singing and saying my prayers, but the distance was still there.

Things were making me uncomfortable. My thoughts had dethroned the Master and wounded Him, but I supposed that if I kept up the appearance of nearness to Christ, I would have

31

it. I lost my appetite for the Bible, which had been a living Book to me, but I kept on reading it anyway as a duty. I should have known that this is a sure sign of spiritual sickness. Prayer became a dull routine and church services were no longer meaningful. I was still trying to be good, but a certain amount of strain had come into my everyday living. I couldn't understand the loneliness I felt...since outwardly nothing had changed. I longed for the old peace.

Then a brother gave a message, after reading Hebrews 10:19-22:

> "Since, therefore, brethren, we have confidence to enter the holy place by the blood of Jesus, by a *new and living way* which He inaugurated for us through the veil, that is, His flesh,...let us draw near with a sincere heart, in full assurance of faith, having our hearts sprinkled clean from an evil conscience...."[1]

The speaker said that this new and living way was for us, the lovers of Jesus, in our everyday living. He talked about the *nearness* and how precious it is—nearness to the Lord and to one another. He said that distances from God and people come easily and are dangerous. I was agreeing. Then he explained that the secret was in having our hearts sprinkled clean from an evil conscience.

A pricking conscience means that the Holy Spirit is trying to deal with you about something. It is possible, he explained, to have an inner voice crying "Unclean, unclean!" as the lepers in Israel used to have to do. This makes you feel utterly alone and in the cold. This is a dangerous area, or an off-limit range, where the enemy can shoot at you at will. I shivered.

He went on to say that the only thing to do was to agree with the Holy Spirit and take that troubled conscience back to the cross where Jesus died. His blood that was shed there is still instantly available for the forgiveness of sins and for the sprinkling of consciences.

In my mind I went back to the day when I had seen Jesus hanging on the cross for me, and remembered that His eyes

32

were full of love as they looked into mine. I cried out in my heart, "Yes, Lord! There is rebellion in my thoughts." I told Him exactly what it was. No sooner did I cry to Him than I knew I was clasped in His arms again.

I was so happy and released that I blurted it to the brethren as soon as the message was over.

They said, "This is what we have been trying to share with you all along. St. Paul taught us, 'As you have therefore received Christ Jesus the Lord, *so walk* in Him.'² How did you receive Him? You turned to Him and trusted Him. You agreed with all He showed you of your sins, and His blood immediately took care of them. They were washed away. So what do you do now when something has made you cold and dry? Exactly the same."

Many years have passed since that day and I have often described what the Lord Jesus and His cross mean to me and the fact that this quick way back into joy has never failed me.

I am not always full of love, not always seeing Him clearly. Self-indulgence has a way of creeping in. Sometimes I am thoroughly empty and have to say so in public. But what I have discovered is that *Jesus loves to fill empties*! All I need to do is to keep open to Him and to admit frankly what's wrong. He does the rest.

This is where "respectable" Christianity fails. God does not deal with respectability; He deals only with reality.

Sometimes I make the mistake that Moses made when he disobeyed the Lord in the desert and struck the rock with his staff instead of speaking to it.³ In his anger at the people he disobeyed God, but he probably rationalized it, saying, "Well, actually, I did rather well. The water came out and the problem is solved. God knew my anger was justified, so I must be all right spiritually. The results prove it."

He may have been justifying himself, but God's miracle of giving water had nothing at all to do with Moses' righteousness or obedience. The water came because the Lord is merciful and had compassion on His people.

Sometimes I see people responding to the Word of the Lord

which I have preached, even if my heart is not quite right. But I don't get away with self-congratulation, and neither did Moses. God took Moses aside as a friend, had some fellowship with him, and told him a few things that had gone wrong between them. He loves me that way, too.

No matter what grace has done for me in the past, I still need to experience daily the power of the cleansing blood of Jesus, God's Son. And that is not easy. It took everything in Jesus; it took all of Heaven; it took Gethsemane and Calvary; it took a pure God with a perfect heart to put His blessed hands into the mess of humanity to make this possible. It is because of the tears, blood and sweat of the cross that the intruding sins can be both forgiven and forgotten.

There is a story about Martin Luther. Even after he had come into a liberating experience with God, he was tempted, and was always merciless with himself over the things he had done or failed to fulfill spiritually.

Once, when he was miserable, a brother said to him, "Martin, God has blessed you, but you have not yet discovered the 'God of the Agains.' You need to know the God who *keeps* on saving you."

Martin listened carefully and then he jumped to his feet. As he later explained it, "I could now say to the Devil, 'What you have accused me of is quite true, and you have left out a few things, but you must now take a red pencil and draw a *cross* through the list, for it is *finished*. I have discovered the God of the Agains!' "

Luther had learned that you can only go up by going down. True, St. Paul says that God "blessed us in Christ with every spiritual blessing in the heavenly places,"[4] and "raised us *up* with him, and made us sit with him in the heavenly places in Christ Jesus."[5] But it is only when we are *down* at His feet that we share His throne. The lower we are the more blessed we are.

God, whose name is Holy, says, "I dwell in the high and holy place, with him also who is of a humble, broken spirit, to revive the spirit of the humble and to revive the heart of the repenting ones.''[6]

Repentance means simply to turn and to agree with God. ''For if we take up the attitude 'we have not sinned,' we flatly deny God's diagnosis of our condition and cut ourselves off from what He has to say to us.''[7] The Holy Spirit is an accurate diagnostician. Those who are in the fellowship of God's people need to learn the art of being His patients in His divine clinic. The patient's responsibility is to cooperate with the Doctor, not to resist Him. Our first and healthy attitude is to say ''Yes'' to His diagnosis.

God is operating on His people to make them like the Son of God, to create His image in them continually. To allow Him to do this, we need to submit to the Holy Spirit. If He says it is a tumor and you say it is only a headache, the healing may be impossible. Whether it is an attitude or an action, sin is sin.

If I say, ''Yes, Lord. You're right,'' then my case is easy. He is faithful and reliable to begin the healing immediately: ''He forgives our sins and makes us thoroughly clean from all that is evil.''[8]

When a hard attitude has invaded my inner man and interrupted the flow of the Holy Spirit, the Comforter is grieved. What do I do? I go to the hospital. God's hospital has one medicine: the love of Jesus Christ. His love breaks me, convicts me, releases me and heals me all at once. There is no gap between repenting and rejoicing.

I meet Christians who think that, after repenting, you have to remain miserable and be punished for a while. We Anglicans have a prayer in our liturgy in which we confess that we are ''miserable offenders,'' and of course we remain miserable as long as we harden our hearts. But we forget that the very moment of turning is the moment of rejoicing. New Testament repentance does not include, as some religions do, a long period of remorse or being put into a sort of spiritual quarantine before you come into grace. That is why you can see a person both weeping and laughing at once.

In Africa I have seen people suddenly touched by God in

35

a meeting, stand to confess, and they are shouting "Hallelujah" at the same time. Why? Because they have turned to the Healer and are already healed.

Turning *from* the sin that made you miserable and *to* the Lord is all one motion. The two are one act, and that is why joy comes instantly.

Remorse without looking to Jesus is dangerous. Judas was filled with remorse and it threw him into a vacuum, into committing spiritual and physical suicide.

Repenting is turning and seeing Jesus. That is what Thomas did on that second Lord's Day.[9] After a week of bitter depression and unbelief, Thomas saw the wounded hands and the outpoured love of the Son of God reaching out to him. Repentance, forgiveness, faith and flooding joy came all in one breath: "My Lord and my God!" Forgiveness and fullness come together.

Another wonderful thing is that God deliberately forgets our past. In the new covenant God made with us, He says, "I will remember their sins and their misdeeds no more."[10] So He does not keep a long record on each of us.

You may come saying, "Lord, I'm sorry to trouble You again with this pride."

And He will reply, "Oh? Were you here before with that?" When He says "It is finished," it is finished.

All this does not mean that He is asking of us a morbid introspection. Not at all. He is the Organist and we are the keys on His keyboard. The time for a key to go down is only when it is touched by the finger of the organist.

An organist would be entirely frustrated if the keys of the organ kept going up and down of their own accord without being touched. They would make a jarring discord.

On the other hand, if a key was stuck and would not go down at his touch, or remained down after his touch, he would have to stop and say, "It is impossible for me to play until this key is fixed."

Or what if one key should speak up and say to the organist, "Wait a minute. Don't touch me, touch this one first"? Again the organist would give up and say, "These keys are in rebellion. I know the piece I want to play and how to produce the harmony. Please, *leave it to me.*"

The Spirit of Jesus knows how to make music. The hand that was nailed to the cross is the only hand qualified to play on the keys of His keyboard. I may be a church minister, but I am not permitted to push your "key" down. Jesus has the tender, wounded hands. See, mine have no wounds. His gentle hands never break a life, but have put many lives together. Respond to *Him.*

Remember, you are a *necessary* key on the keyboard, without which the music cannot be played. Say to Him, "Yes, Master, touch me when and where You want; I trust Your hands of love. As you touch me I see that I have an unclean conscience, but I bow now in repentance. Cleanse and wash me. Thank you, Master, I am up again. Was it Your hand that made the beautiful music I heard just now?"

Jesus is at the organ, and when He is free to touch each one of us when He chooses, there is harmony, thrilling music, a concert for all the world to hear.

- - - - - -

1   *NASV.*
2   Colossians 2:6, *NKJV.*
3   Numbers 20:7-13.
4   Ephesians 1:3, *RSV.*
5   Ephesians 2:6, *RSV.*
6   Isaiah 57:15, translation from Kiswahili.
7   1 John 1:10, *Phillips.*
8   1 John 1:9, *Phillips.*
9   John 20:26-29.
10 Hebrews 10:17, *RSV.*

CHAPTER 5

Love's Togetherness

That evening, when I found that Calvary love was mine, a second surprise was to find that I was enfolded into a loving family of people of all sorts who cared deeply for one another and for me. The Lord Jesus was at the center of each of their lives and in the center of their love-fellowship. They were human and imperfect and frequently failed, but they knew the quick way back into restoration and praise.

As they told me, Jesus laid the foundation for this togetherness of theirs on the night when He was betrayed. He knew He was leaving His disciples very soon, and while He was longing for them to be deeply united, He also knew that there was strife and jealousy among them. St. Luke lets us in on it by saying, "They began to argue among themselves as to who would have the highest rank."[1] The atmosphere was tense; these men were scowling. Not one of them was sharing Christ's vision of His redeeming work or of their part in taking it to the world.

How could He leave the Church in their hands? What could He do? Disqualify them? Give them up? No, because as St. John said, "He loved them unto the furthermost limits of love."[2]

In the presence of these men, each greedy for recognition, the Master, the Guest of Highest Honor, rose from His place, stripped off His outer garment, tied a towel around His waist like a slave, poured water into a basin, and knelt at the feet of one of His disciples.

What an embarrassment to that self-centered crowd! In their

arguing, no one had remembered the common courtesy of water for washing.

Then the Lord Jesus, who had stilled the waves and raised the dead, asked for the feet of the first disciple. Another shock! He waited. Feet weren't respectable to Jews, but He did not ask for a respectable part. He wanted the feet, dusty from the road. Each one thought, "Oh, my dirty feet! And He is the Lord of Heaven."

Of course, when He came to Simon Peter, Peter objected, "Master, You shouldn't be washing my feet like this!"

Jesus replied, "You don't understand now why I am doing it, but someday you will, Peter."

"No!" he protested, "You shall *never* wash my feet!"

"But if I don't, you can't be My partner."

That was a bomb, but Peter made a quick recovery: "Then wash my hands and head as well—not just my feet."

"No," Jesus replied. "One who has bathed all over needs only to have his feet washed to be entirely clean." Now the gaze of everyone was riveted on Him. Their strife was forgotten, the atmosphere had changed. Not one of them could claim that he didn't need to be washed. They were all alike. Suddenly, all were partners with Him...and also joined to one another.

My new brothers told me, "We are united as long as the gaze of each one is fixed on Him, and as long as we allow Him daily to wash our dirty feet." For us, the dust from the road is the wrong reactions, the unkind words, the selfish pride and all such. Only after being washed can we see each other in love and look outside to those whom He wants to liberate.

I was nurtured in a close-knit community of the "footwashed." In those days we met together every day after work. We sat facing each other in a circle, young and old, men and women, educated and illiterate, each one precious to all the others.

We were very conscious that Jesus Himself was in the midst of us, and we were listening to Him. We devoured His words in the Bible with full expectation that He would show us in it what He wanted us to do. It was our only book then and we came to it without preconceptions. No wonder He could speak so clearly through it.

After the reading, whoever gained an insight on what had been read shared it. It might be a little girl of ten or an old man of seventy saying what the words meant to her or him. I have received some of the deepest spiritual insights from old ladies who had never been to school. They listen carefully to the Word as it is read, it goes in, and they bring out some precious things because they are in fellowship with the Author and know what is in His heart.

Every day, when we reached a consensus on what the Holy Spirit was teaching us to do, there was deep heart-searching and frequently some repentance. There was also joy. We sang a lot. The music came out of realizing that God had spoken and that we had gladly chosen to obey.

It was in this atmosphere that we were transparent with each other, knowing that we were loved and instantly forgiven by the brethren when we were forgiven by God. It was reassuring to me, after telling them what God had dealt with in me, to have them celebrate the forgiveness by lifting a praise chorus. With them, as with God, the past was forgiven and forgotten. No one ever brought it up again. We came to know each other well, as sinners together at the foot of the cross. Down there we felt free to share anything.

This unity gave direction and power to prayer. By the time we were ready to pray, we knew what to pray for and wasted no time in having to clear away hindrances. No wonder we saw God moving.

For one thing, He kept sending us out. We went, whether we were invited or not, on foot, an assorted "ad hoc" team spilling over into neighboring valleys, usually leaving "Jesus people" behind when we came back home. Ordinary folk, bound together in a true love-fellowship, can be a powerhouse for evangelism.

In the more than forty years since God's moving power began in our part of Africa we have seen communities of fellowship grow in most of the cities, towns, and hamlets of East Africa. There is a grapevine that has kept all these small and large groups in touch with one another. By travelers, by letters, by local and wider gatherings, news of the gospel is spread. I still marvel at hearing repeated in a remote village a message that stirred a large convention hundreds of miles away.

There are also places around the world to which sparks of fire have spread, and people have come from every continent to see what God is doing in East Africa. Visitors who have attended the great conventions, when up to thirty thousand people gather to praise God, have referred to these as being the "East Africa revival," without realizing that the conventions are just an overflow from the steady, day-by-day discipline of the open-hearted fellowship going on in hundreds of places even today.

St. Paul's instructions were: "Open your hearts to one another as Christ has opened his heart to you, and God will be glorified."[3] Jesus shared deeply and without reserve with His disciples; otherwise we would not know in such detail about the temptations when He was alone in the wilderness. The purpose of our being open with one another is so that God may be glorified, and so that His shining character may come out. And what is His character? "God is love."[4] And how do we know this unique love? By the fact that "Christ laid down his life for us." And how does this affect us? "We ought to lay down our lives for the brethren."[5]

I have seen many methods devised in attempting to produce a love-fellowship. But the only known power for keeping together a group of believers—intact in love, fruitful and not ingrown—is the presence of the Author in the midst who is listened to and obeyed. It is not a product of man's desire for socializing. It is a fruit of Christ's self-giving love, which always draws us together and creates a community wherever people have opened their hearts to Him.

When the Lord is in the midst, the Holy Spirit makes us alert and sensitive to each other's needs. This is what the prophet calls "the heart of flesh" in place of a cold, stony heart.[6] The Spirit is the One who sets us "free to serve one another in love."[7] This serving is done in practical ways which are visible to onlookers. There were many in Uganda, and eventually in all East Africa, who echoed the words of the pagan Romans which Tertullian tells us about, "Behold these Christians, how they love one another!"

A widow whose house is in disrepair may find the believers together building a new one for her. A hungry family may find a bag of grain at the door in the morning. A young person may find that his school fees have been paid. No doubt the loving-kindness and hospitality of the brethren has attracted many to "join" them, who later found that this brotherhood was far costlier than they were prepared for.

Every time you ask forgiveness it takes a little dying, and so also does submitting one to another in the fear of God.[8] But both are liberating. For instance, I soon wanted to give up teaching and do nothing but run around testifying to the Calvary love I had seen and was experiencing. God let me keep telling it, but my brothers, firmly and wisely, kept me in the schoolroom for twenty years, saying, "Festo, for now, just keep on teaching." What a good thing that was! I had so many lessons to learn before becoming a full-time evangelist.

Now, as an evangelist and bishop, I am still learning and finding His lessons of submission important. I have thanked God through the years for His faithful ones who have been willing to obey the Lord Jesus' command: "If I then, your Lord and Teacher, have washed your feet, you also ought to wash one another's feet."[9]

Recently I was coming from my cathedral feeling that I had preached a good sermon. Then a dear lady, about seventy years old, illiterate, one of those saints with a sensitive spirit, took my hand and thanked me for the message. Very quietly she added, "Bishop, what is wrong? You sounded rather dry." There was no tone of despising or criticism in her voice, only redeeming love. Before I could answer, she said, "Just take it to the Lord,'' and went on her way.

So down on my face at home I took it to Him. She was right. He needed to show me the thing that was hindering the flow of the Spirit.

To be living in a community of New Testament openness is to be renewed, rebuked, challenged, refilled, and to find that the burden of one is lifted by all.

- - - - - -

1 Luke 22:24, *LB*.
2 John 13:1, free translation from the Greek.
3 Romans 15:7, *Phillips*.
4 1 John 4:16.
5 1 John 3:16.
6 Ezekiel 36:26.
7 Galatians 5:13, *Phillips*.
8 Ephesians 5:21.
9 John 13:14, *NKJV*.

CHAPTER 6

Love on the Throne

Look around the circle. Each person is seemingly concentrating on the Lord Jesus. They have evidently forgotten whether the one on the other side is black or white, a man or a woman, very young or very old, clergyman, bishop, graduate or unlearned, housewife or errand boy.

All are listening to messages from the Lord. All are free to share. All are letting the light of God's holy Word shine into their lives.

St. John told us about this. He said that if we walk in the light—that is, in the presence of God, as Jesus Christ Himself is always in the presence of the Father—then we have fellowship with one another.[1] He is almost saying that when we fulfill these conditions, *we cannot help having fellowship* with one another.

So what does it mean to "walk in the light"?

The light of His presence and His written Word shines into you first. It brings to light the things which are not like Jesus, so they can be cleansed. Then your heart is free.

Then His light shines on your brother, making him precious. That does not mean he is perfect. If I demand perfection, by whose standard is he to be perfect? My standard? How miserable and monotonous!

To have fellowship is not to have uniformity. It is the drawing presence of Jesus Christ, the Light of God, penetrating me and shining on my brother so that we inevitably are drawn toward each other, and into fellowship.

What makes it possible for us to go on walking and working together peacefully? St. John tells the secret: "... and the blood of Jesus Christ, God's Son, keeps on cleansing us from all sin."[1] The Spirit of God continually applies the death of Christ to cleanse out the things which break the fellowship of God's people. This is not to make us miserable, but rather to make us happy. When something comes up between us, it makes it possible for us to come back together again, to ask each other's forgiveness and to start again. This time our fellowship is deeper.

We cannot claim to be different from the disciples in the upper room who were arguing about which of them would have the highest rank. There is something in human nature that keeps wanting to climb ladders, no matter what spiritual gifts and experiences we have. For example, take this not unusual instance.

A pastor was standing in a small meeting of intimate brethren. He is convicted of having set himself on a pedestal and is weeping. He tells us:

"I would go up into my pulpit with my big Bible and give God's message with fervor. People often responded and I figured I was doing a good job. I climbed higher and higher until I was on a little throne, but rather conspicuous and telling everyone what to do. People would come to me for help, but me—I seemingly had no need. I have been giving the impression that I am unique and untroubled by the flesh. But it isn't true! The Holy Spirit has shown me my heart. He has told me that I am simply a little clay vessel through whom He wants to communicate His treasures. When I became more than that, I was out of place, and His blessing dried up. Forgive me, brothers, this has made you suffer too."

When he finishes what he has to say, joy breaks out in a chorus around him. We are all on our feet singing and embracing him. One clergyman, especially, who recently learned that the only place of power is down low at the Lord Jesus' feet, stands with his brother and puts his arms around him understandingly.

Several times during the past thirty or forty years, the peace of the East African fellowship has been disturbed by ladder-climbing and division, usually temporary. It happens when someone or some small group claims more perfection than others, or takes control. The stand they take sounds good: "I have more zeal," or "I have abandoned all worldly possessions," or "I am more strict in holiness in things like haircuts or charge accounts...so come, follow me, and separate yourself from the others." It is hard to resist.

The cure for such "climbing" (and it really works) is in seeing again my need for the grace of God and falling before Him, as Joshua did.

After the death of Moses, Joshua had assumed command of the People of God; in fact, he had been called to it. But perhaps he was taking a little credit for their success in crossing the Jordan. At any rate, now he was looking over the walls of Jericho, planning his strategy of war.[2]

Joshua looked up and suddenly, "behold, there stood a man right in front of him with his sword drawn in his hand." He was a stranger, obviously a soldier, and ready to fight. It was a confrontation.

Joshua did what any brave soldier would do. Without retreating, he went straight forward, demanding, "Are you for us or are you for our enemies?"

The Man answered, "No! But as Commander of the army of the Lord have I come!"

What a shock. Joshua looked on himself as the commander. Was he dismissed? Yes, as a matter of fact, he was fired on the spot, for Another had come to take over. Joshua was no longer in command. And it was a good thing. Otherwise the People of God would have suffered defeat, as the fiasco at Ai proved.[3]

Recognition came to Joshua, and he "fell on his face to the earth and did worship, and said to him, 'What saith my Lord unto his servant?' "

There he took the leader's rightful place. The man who thought he would lead on to victory was himself conquered first. In a few days the walls of Jericho were going to fall

47

down, but the leader had to fall first. This is always God's order.

After that, no doubt, Joshua expected to learn how to mobilize the people and get things done. But, instead, the new Commander said, "Put off your shoes, Joshua, from off your feet, for the place on which you are is holy ground."

Was that irrelevant? It seemed to have nothing to do with Jericho. But the Lord was saying, "*Jericho* is not My problem, Joshua. *You* are. I know what to do with Jericho, but first I need to deal with you. If you are going to work in fellowship with Me, and win Canaan, I have to teach you who I Am. Moses learned this lesson at the burning bush, but you need to learn it. You are trying to be a warrior without first falling at My feet. You must learn the holiness of My Presence, and that the secret of victory is a cleansed heart. Take off those shoes."

The shoes may have symbolized some spiritual pride, or maybe there was something else. At any rate, Joshua fell down before the Lord, took off his shoes. . .and a week later the walls of Jericho fell down.

In East Africa these days, the Lord has been asking us to "take off our shoes" by repenting of unlove. Walls were built through disobedience to His command to "love one another as I have loved you." Down at His feet love has returned, and walls are falling.

Any group that is committed to walking and working together in love is in God's workshop. The Holy Spirit has tools and equipment to bring each important part into shape. There are those who think they are big, who suffer from a superiority complex. These, along with the ones who think they are little, who suffer from an inferiority complex, all need to be made one size—His size.

You know that if the ball bearings in the hub of a bicycle wheel are exactly the same size, the wheel runs smoothly. If you put unequal bearings in the wheel, there is a crunching sound and you go nowhere on that bicycle. The Lord is continually in the process of filing down and building up His "ball bearings.''

He wants us to accept each other as human beings, like ourselves, no better, no worse. Each is frail; in all of us the flesh tries to interfere with what God is doing, and the Enemy tries to insert some darkness. We know by experience that ''if we say that we have fellowship with [God] while we walk in darkness, we lie and do not live according to the truth.''[4]

It is only by doggedly and persistently staying in the place of a sinner needing grace that we can avoid succumbing to the tactics of the Enemy of our souls. Satan knows that if he can encourage in one of us a little pride with a touch of ambition to be the one at the top of the heap, he can woo him away from love and from feeling the need for the cross. He may urge this leader to preach impassioned sermons, usually a bit too loud, and will give him all the Scripture verses he needs to ''prove his position.'' All this will accomplish the Enemy's purpose of dethroning the ONLY ONE who has a right to be on the Throne.

I have seen Satan use even beautiful spiritual gifts to trip God's people. I was once with a group of lovely folk and some of them had been speaking in tongues. The Spirit of God came upon them and they spoke heavenly words. What a great experience! Like third heaven. Then, do you know what happened? The flesh came in slowly and these began to think they were better than others, making the others feel like second-class Christians.

Fellowship was interrupted, bitterness and aloofness emerged. The Holy Spirit was obstructed because a strange spirit had penetrated the community of God's people. The good gift of the Father, through the Spirit, had been taken advantage of by the flesh and misused to the detriment of Christ's Body. They needed to come down, repent and be cleansed, not of the gift, which was holy, but of the wrong use made of it.

My brother, Dr. Joe Church, has an unusual way of picturing things. This is the way he puts it:

''God is wise and knows us well. I think He says, 'Yes, today they are saved. They are born again and filled with My

Spirit. Wait till tomorrow. Some will be fighting among themselves. But I will make provision to recover the situation when that happens. I am going to see that the death of My almighty Son, the living Christ, is available to be applied to those dear ones for their renewal. When tensions come between brother and brother, misunderstandings of any kind, or criticisms, I will lead them back to where it all began.' "

Dr. Church continues: "So the Holy Spirit comes into a group that is tense, where you find it difficult to breathe. They are singing, but with hearts that are cold. There is no flowing together. The Spirit looks around. He finds one who is willing. (You know that we are not all willing at the same time.) He takes that one to Calvary's cross, puts His hand on the back of his neck, saying, 'Kneel and bow here.' Then, leaning down, He whispers, 'Please stay here till I come back.'

"Then He goes back into the group and brings another, makes him or her kneel and says, 'Please remain here.' The line becomes longer and now each one is saying, 'Father, forgive *me* (not forgive them!), forgive my attitude, my hardness, my sharp words.' There is no more pointing of fingers, for all are in the presence of the love of Christ.

"By the time they look up, praising, all are there. There is no longer any division, but glad embracing of each other."

I have seen this happen and have been a part of it again and again. It is beautiful. Right now God is doing a work like this in East Africa, and it is good.

Once a team of us were speaking in the delightful country of Burundi at a time when there were deep intertribal enmities. The Spirit of God was piercing that darkness with the redeeming love of Jesus.

One man was released. He crossed the room weeping, stood beside a brother and touched him on the shoulder. By that time this man was also in tears. He stood up and they embraced each other. They both at once began asking for forgiveness. They had studied together for two years and were about to be ordained to the ministry, but they had not loved each other because they were of hostile tribes.

Something like electric power was released in that room, and most of the people there got rid of their resentments and hatreds that day. The reconciliations lasted through the bitter days of turmoil that followed in that country.

I have known people to become fearful of openhearted fellowship because it has been said by someone, "Well, I don't believe in hanging my dirty linen on the line for the neighbors to see!"

Neither do we. What we share with one another is spotlessly clean linen, and it is a joy to "hang it out." God has already washed it thoroughly, or is at that instant making it clean. Sharing with our brothers and sisters—of course, within limits of being brief and circumspect—about what God has delivered us from, has frequently been used by the Holy Spirit to reveal to someone else a blind spot or a forgotten closet needing attention. Moreover, it draws us close together, reminding us that we are all alike and all the same size.

This is entirely different from the custom of some groups to sit and lay out before each other all their hang-ups and angers, then pick them all up and go home with them. That *is* displaying dirty linen.

Sharing in Jesus is liberating and gives one a sense of fresh start. The Lord Jesus, the Healing One, is in the center, and through the sharing shows us what to pray for one another and ways of serving one another.

One sad thing can happen. When, in the light of God, I have been convicted that something has gone wrong, if my pride reacts to the gentle Voice, the Devil may be able to push it too far and take it over as his accusation. He then starts nagging and telling me I am hopeless.

"You'll never make it," he jeers. "You are too bad to walk with Jesus. You can never overcome that habit or change your personality. You know God is holy and expects perfection. You might as well give up." And on and on. He preaches despair, despondency and depression, and surprisingly enough, sometimes I listen to him instead of to the Saviour. I take his advice and spend silly hours lamenting and hating myself, as if the Saviour were too distant to give me a helping hand.

But Jesus is much nearer than I realize at times like that, and He is instantly ready whenever I begin to turn toward Him, whether it is on my bed, or on the road, or anywhere else.

My brethren are quick to recognize the voice of the Enemy. So if I, or anyone else, is repeating the bad news of the Enemy which denies the love of God and the power of the cross, they quietly but quite firmly say, "Shetani! [Satan!]" Recognizing Satan, as Jesus did in Peter,[5] and calling him by name, strips him of his weapons. He becomes like the roaring lion in Bunyan's *Pilgrim's Progress* who was chained and unable to touch Pilgrim as long as he stayed on the path.

It is dangerous to cover up sin before the Lord.

Joseph's ten brothers did so for a long time. They had sold their own brother into slavery, which was close to murder. They had to tell lies and labor under the deception for eighteen years.

Then, graciously, God brought them to Joseph whom they had sold.[6] They would have dreaded to see him, but they were forced by circumstances. Some of us are forced by circumstances to stand before Another whom we have hurt, One who is greater than Joseph.

They didn't recognize Joseph, the ruler of Egypt, but he knew them. He looked into their eyes and knew they were feeling guilty. He spoke to them through an interpreter, and because he loved them, he did not reveal himself to them. He hoped they would be willing to bring the old thing out, bury it, and relieve their consciences of misery.

For a long time they evaded the truth.

Joseph said, "You are spies!"

That was a harsh word, they thought, and it made them try to explain themselves. They said:

"We are true men. [Were they?] Thy servants are twelve brethren. [That was true, and good counting.] We are sons of one man in the land of Canaan [True], and behold the youngest is this day with his father [True], and one is not. [False! Where was he?]"

It was an unnecessary confession, but something compelled them to bring it up. And why did they lie in the last phrase about Joseph? Probably because it was haunting them.

I have heard people who are praying in long sessions for revival. Sometimes they make long "confessions" right up to the point of the thing that is haunting them. God is waiting for them to tell Him the truth, but there they stop.

Joseph was waiting for the truth too. If they could have ended their story by saying, ". . . and the other one we sold into slavery," what a shortcut that would have been!

There is a confession, a general admitting that something is wrong, which nevertheless leaves us safe and spares us the cross. It has happened sometimes in our fellowship meetings. When a person thinks he has learned the "technique" but has not been forgiven, he tells a long story, smoothing it over with psychological words that imply he has been unfortunate but is not really guilty, needing grace. Truth is evaded and no liberation follows.

Now see Joseph's brothers talking to one another by themselves: "We are guilty concerning our brother in that we saw the anguish of his soul when he besought us and we would not hear; therefore is this distress come upon us." They could admit it to themselves, but not where it was needed, that is, to Jacob and Joseph.

There are men who gossip freely about trouble with their wives, and wives who gossip about their husbands, but they can't go straight to Jesus and the person concerned. In front of the offended ones, they put on borrowed smiles. They are "spies"—that is, those who look to be what they are not.

So the brothers of Joseph became more and more distressed. Why has distress come upon our homes, our businesses, our offices and our churches? It may be that God has taken away the blessing until we stop evading the truth.

The brothers blamed Joseph, saying, "The lord of the land spoke roughly with us!" Rough, is he? Do rough people turn aside and weep? Joseph was a tenderhearted man, but he had to permit them to suffer until they came to the end of their

53

cover-up. You may be giving your precious soul a rough time unnecessarily by not admitting the truth. Many, many Christians need to have the masks they wear taken away by the Holy Spirit. Those are miserable deceptions.

Finally, the time came when Judah was on his face before Joseph, crying, "What shall we say to my lord?...Or how shall we clear ourselves? God has found out the iniquity of your servants...."[7] That is exactly what Joseph was waiting for, and when Judah finished speaking he could reveal to them who he was—their lost brother.

Jesus Christ, whom you betrayed, has not moved an inch from where He has been waiting for you—at Calvary.

- - - - - -

[1] 1 John 1:7, personal paraphrase.
[2] Joshua 5:13-15.
[3] Joshua 7:1-5.
[4] 1 John 1:6, *RSV*.
[5] Matthew 16:23.
[6] Genesis 42:9 and on.
[7] Genesis 44:16, *NKJV*.

CHAPTER 7

Love Comes Home

Nowhere is openhearted fellowship more difficult, more important or more beautiful than at home.

As a young single teacher, when I came into the family of God, I was frequently invited into the homes of those who had begun to walk the Way before me. I saw homes full of light that made a deep impression on me.

It was an amazing thing to me to see what dignity and freedom of spirit the Lord had brought to the women of God. African men are often polygamous and traditionally they like to be treated as chiefs in their homes, with their wives as mere slaves. But here I saw a husband giving a place of honor to his wife, and watched her fill the place competently as a beloved equal in the sight of the Lord. I even saw a man kneel down before his wife and say, "I have been mean and hurtful to you, my dear. I am sorry. Please forgive me."

I had never imagined it possible for a man to consult with his wife on business matters, but here was a wage earner who took his salary home and laid it out intact on the table so that he and his wife together might pray and seek the will of the Lord in its use.

Before dawn every morning, the families who loved Jesus would rise and wash, gather in a room and begin to sing praises to the Lord. Each morning, when I woke, I could hear the singing rise from one nearby home after another. Then I knew they were reading the Scripture Union portion[1] for the day, and meditating on it together. This would lead into a sharing of what the Lord was speaking to any one of the family, a free time to talk over the plans or problems of the day and a period of trusting, earnest prayer. This became the new tradition and it spread all over East Africa as the way in which a Jesus home begins the day.

We unmarried people were often included in one or another of the families for our instruction. Much was said to us about God's plan for marriage, that it was intended to complete one's life, just as God gave Eve to Adam as "a helper in harmony with him."[2] We were told that husbands are to love their wives in the way that Christ loves His Bride, the Church, doing all He can to bring her to perfection.[3]

What we saw was a new order of mutual respect and self-giving, with the Lord Jesus Christ in the center. I began to dream of establishing my own home.

Three years after I began to walk with Jesus and with my new Christian family, they agreed with me that the time was right to think of marriage. When I spoke to Mera, the beautiful young teacher who had my heart, I knew that the brothers and sisters were with me in loving concern and would rejoice with me that she had accepted my proposal. They arranged for us a wedding full of the joy of the Lord, which amazed my relatives and hers and gave us a splendid opportunity to tell them about the One whom we planned to make the focus of our new home.

Mera had begun to walk with the Lord several years before I did and had gone through some persecution at boarding school for her forthright testimony. We have been married now for over thirty-five years, our four daughters are grown, and we have learned many things together. I thank God for Mera. She is the best chaplain I have. Each of us needs one or two people who minister to us spiritually, and she is the best for me, because she knows me intimately.

As is usual for two people who love one another at close quarters, there are times when things sneak in between us which may be meaningless, but which are not like Jesus. When they do creep in, do you know what I do? We have an insect in Africa which curls up when you touch it. I am like that.

Too often, when something goes wrong at home, I turn in on myself and keep quiet, hoping that my wife will not detect it. But she does. Thank God, she does.

We both know that we are grieving the Holy Spirit when we sit on something that is unforgiven. My wife's ministry is a gentle word that turns my eyes away from my misery to see again the pure light of Jesus' face and to kneel down at His cross.

She knows when I have a problem. She knows when I am hard. She knows when I am depressed and she knows how to help me. Sometimes when I preach, she afterwards takes me aside and says, "Festo, as you were preaching today, you made too much noise. People could not get all the words."

Or another day she may say, "Festo, you are wearing a frown. Is there something wrong? Let us go to Jesus together." I may thank God and be healed. Or I may pull back, swell up and begin thinking, "Am I not the head of this house? Why should she speak to me like that? She is just impossible."

When that happens, I get more and more puffed up until finally I am like a big balloon. A balloon's emptiness of all but air reminds me of the New Testament word that means, "empty glory."[4] I am inflated with myself, thinking that the bigger I am the better. I act as if I were saying, "Now, everyone bow down to me!"

I get fussy with the children. They bump into my balloon and it bounces them away. Of course, when the children bounce away they become like balloons too and soon the whole home is full of inflated human beings. In the evening I take my Bible, while I am still inflated, and call the family together for prayers. My wife comes, poor thing; she has been bounced off and is becoming inflated. My children come, resenting me. In that condition, is there any fellowship in our home?

How in the world is the Holy Spirit going to draw this family together? It isn't easy. But in one way or anothher, using the sharp point of His Word, the Saviour gets ready to prick one of the balloons. My problem is that I think my wife ought to be deflated first, but the Holy Spirit knows better. He is just and good and will deal only with me concerning what is wrong with *me*, not on what I think is wrong with someone else.

When He pricks a balloon...whoooosh! One of us truly asks for forgiveness and that balloon is limp, and then others also get tender and approachable and we can relate, communicate, and understand each other again.

You know how the hinges of a door can get rusty, and when someone opens the door, it squeaks loudly. In our home, when patience or flexibility is growing thin, we squeak. I hear my voice going up and up. This makes the children squeak too. We need oil. When the Spirit of Christ puts His oil on the hinges, our voices are natural again, hearts beating in tune.

God put the first young couple in a lovely place, the Garden of Eden. He had created them in His own image, both of them, so the conversation was cheerful. No harshness, resentments, suspicions or jealousies were there. Life was full and joy complete because God was in the center. When we walk in His way, we relive this Eden life to a degree.

Then Adam and Eve decided to take freedom into their own hands and they jumped over the fence of God's protective limitation. Seeking something better than God, they lost all. They were no longer comfortable with the Creator. He became a threat and they took to hiding.

But God came to the hiding ones. In love, He said, "Adam, where are you?"[5]

That doesn't mean that God is ignorant. He is simply saying, "Adam, you are completely in the wrong place, and where is your dear Eve? What has happened? Have you eaten the wrong thing?"

Adam should have said, "Yes, Lord. I'm sorry. I was really wrong."

Instead, he complained: "*That woman....*" He doesn't call her "dear" or "honey," he doesn't even call her by name. "That woman, whom You gave me...." You gave me the wrong one, Lord. It's *Your* fault, really. This woman is guilty and You are guilty, so I am the least guilty of all!

When you point an accusing finger at your partner, watch out! Three fingers of that hand will be pointing back at you.

Let me be practical. One day my wife and I were preparing for a weekend spiritual conference. In the evening we sat discussing the things we were going to take in the car. It went well until she suggested one thing, and I said, "No, I don't think we need that, dear."

I thought she would say, "Fine, darling." Instead, she explained why we needed it. I explained why we didn't. The more we talked, the farther apart we got. Finally it got late. I stacked my guns and she stacked hers. Our brief prayers were meaningless and we went to bed.

She slept, bless her, but I didn't sleep.

About midnight, the Holy Spirit called me, "Festo!"

And I said, "Yes, Lord?"

"You aren't sleeping."

"No, Lord."

"And of course you are very holy and your wife is a sinner. Does that mean that when people are holy they don't sleep? Or is it because you have a burden for you wife?... Aren't you really accusing her? And aren't you wasting My time? You wasted the prayer time, you put your wife in the cold, and you are just miserable. You were unnecessarily hard. Now no more talk."

I said, "Yes, Lord. What shall I do?"

"You must ask for forgiveness."

"Now, Lord?"

"No, no. In the morning."

So in the morning I said, "Dear, I'm sorry. It was I who caused that terrible patch of darkness. Please forgive me."

Bless her, she forgave me and said, "No, it was my fault. I was unnecessarily fussy."

Light came into our darkness as peace came back. We embraced and sang in the bedroom and then went outside to put things in the car. When she put that thing in, I wondered why I had argued over it, and we both went rejoicing in the Lord.

At the conference, the Spirit said, "Tell the people about

59

it." I did, and He broke into lives and mended some nearly broken homes that day.

One man said, "I don't know what has happened to my wife. She looks so beautiful now!" True, she was smiling, but she looked the same to us. He had changed.

One day a little girl, who was watching her mother working in the kitchen, asked, "Mummy, what does God do all day long?"

For a while her mother was stumped, but then she said, "Darling, I'll tell you what God does all day long. He spends His whole day mending broken things."

Perhaps you think yours is a situation which will never get mended. I have spoken to people who say, "You don't understand. If you knew the circumstances in which I find myself, you would know that they can never be changed! Things have really gone too far. You don't know my husband (or my wife, or my teenager), do you?"

This always reminds me of how Martha of Bethany felt when she said, "If only you had been here, Lord, my brother would never have died."[6] But now the situation is hopeless. He has been dead four days.

Jesus knew the situation perfectly and He knew what He would do. First, He needed to go to the bottom of the problem, and He said, "Where have you laid him?"

Can we say with Martha, "Come and see"? Come, Lord, look into my home life. It is not all respectable, but come anyway.

And "Jesus wept." They were tears of love and understanding. He knows our heartaches. When He looks into a situation, and when He is given permission, He never leaves it as He found it.

He even wanted to look into the grave. That was hard. Repenting is not easy, and some things are smellier than others, causing grief. But take heart! Open it up. Out of that stinking grave came glory. He may be saying to you, "Only trust Me when it is 'hopeless' and you will see the glory of God come out of your situation too."

It is easy to cause a wound, but hard to heal it. If God did not intervene with grace, we would all be reckoned as murderers. One day I used an expression that cut the heart out of my dear wife and caused a wound there.

When I thought of going to the kitchen to ask forgiveness, I couldn't do it. A real confession that is not superficial is tough, and of course preachers are supposed to be holy. It is a fact that the higher one is the more difficult it is to come down. Besides, I argued, it was her fault. She provoked me.

So coldness grew and my wife seemed a stranger. There was a wall between us—not so thick that we hated each other, just thick enough that we couldn't smile. I had time to draw up a long list of her faults, but in the end it made me miserable.

Jesus knew I was lonely and that the Spirit was grieved, so He began His gracious work. It was Sunday morning when He said to me, "Please give Me your list."

I objected, "But, Lord, she did this and acted that way."

"Yes, I know, but come along. I want to set you free."

"Yes, Lord."

"All right. Now let's look at the list of *your* sins."

Then I found that my list was longer than hers, and Jesus cleansed my sins with His blood.

"Now go to the kitchen where your wife is feeling cold and tell her."

"Yes, Lord, but not right now. I have no time. I have to go and preach in the church. People are waiting for me."

"Fine. You go with your notes and preach, but I will stay in the kitchen with your wife."

That made it very difficult, because without Him preaching is a dry exercise. The Bible does not speak and words don't come. So what is the use of preaching like that? I was actually going out the door when the Holy Spirit turned me around.

"Go to the kitchen."

So I went and said to my wife, "I'm sorry. I caused the quarreling. I was critical and made the Lord sad. It made you a stranger. Please forgive me."

Usually she forgives me quickly, but that time she didn't.

She thought I was doing it just because I wanted to preach well, and so she just shrugged her shoulders.

The Lord said, "Do it again. Let it go deeper. You are not broken enough. You are expecting to be forgiven quickly." Only Jesus always forgives you quickly. Let other people take their time so the Holy Spirit can speak further. And when forgiveness comes, it is sweet.

Finally, when she did forgive me, we sang the Glory song and embraced in the kitchen—it was one of those times we call a "re-wedding." When I hurried to the church, she went with me.

On the way, the Holy Spirit said, "Tell the people in church about it, please." That was hard, but I did, and God opened the windows of Heaven to us that day. Misunderstandings were made right. Repentance came as a gift to many that day.

In and of myself I can't be real. It frightens me. It embarrasses me. But when I go down to the foot of the cross and meet Jesus there, His grace covers my sin, forgives my weaknesses and allows me to be what I am—a forgiven man.

In the atmosphere of mutual forgiveness, and in the provision that Jesus Christ has made for us, Mera and I have discovered that through self-forgetting and self-sacrificing is born a truly creative love. Instead of one emptying the other person for one's own need, each fulfills the other, making him or her more of a person, having more dignity. It brings out the latent qualities in the other, and it partakes somewhat of the love of Christ, who loves His Bride into perfection.

- - - - - -

[1] Scripture Union is an organization based in England which provides a printed plan for reading the Bible through the year, together with notes.

[2] Genesis 2:18, personal paraphrase.

[3] Ephesians 5:25-30.

[4] Galatians 5:26, "vain glory."

[5] Genesis 3:1-12.

[6] John 11:21, *Phillips*.

CHAPTER 8

Love Enables

Calvary love is amazing, for it has been enabling us, as brothers and sisters, to learn many new lessons through the years.

The moving of the Holy Spirit in East Africa, of which I became a part in 1940, began ten years earlier. At first there were just two: Simeoni Nsibambi and Dr. Joe Church. They found each other by God's "accident" near Kampala, Uganda, when both were spiritually hungry to desperation. They dropped everything and sat together under a tree on Namirembe Hill studying the New Testament for days to find out more about the Holy Spirit. He found them, and led them to the cross of Christ and to a simple way of accepting its power daily for continuous personal reviving.

They caught fire. So did Simeoni's brother, Blasio, who accompanied Dr. Joe back to his hospital at Gahini, Rwanda. There, among others, a senior medical assistant, Yosiya Kinuka, came alive and the fire began to spread. It was also spreading in Buganda where Simeoni worked. William Nagenda, a young government clerk, was one whom the Lord touched, together with some other young fellows.

Lawrence Barham, senior missionary in my Kigezi District, mustered enough courage to invite a preaching team from Gahini to Kabale in 1935. He gathered all the boarding school children, the teachers, the evangelists, and the church members to listen. I was one of the youngsters in the boarding school.

Blasio, Dr. Joe, and Yosiya were part of that team. Our attention was riveted by the shining faces of these men who

63

obviously had spiritual freedom, were in love with God, and at peace with one another. We listened, wide-eyed, to what they had to say.

Nothing big happened during those meetings, though one or two were set free. It was too new and startling for most people. But a spiritual bomb had been planted. Within a month, people began to weep unexpectedly, dream dreams of Heaven, or cry out under conviction until they came to know Christ personally. My boarding school was one of the places that was shaken up. That was when I first made the start which I subsequently abandoned. I suppose I was about fourteen years old.

By 1939, when I returned from the Bishop Tucker Memorial College, Mukona, the church in Rukungiri, my home town in northern Kigezi District, had been visited by its share of unexpected occurrences.

What happened first was that on an ordinary Sunday morning a layman stood to read the regularly set Scripture lesson for the day in an ordinary Anglican church. As he was reading, people began to weep. Young people, old men and leading members of the church were affected. The designated preacher never had a chance to preach that day. Tears kept flowing as people saw their sins. When he finished, the man who was reading broke down too.

An hour or so later, most of those still in the church—some had gone home—were on their feet singing. People were embracing after asking each other for forgiveness. Others were still kneeling. The following Sunday the congregation was doubled and the building was too small, so they met outside under the trees.

That was the beginning, and it was some months after that that I came home to teach and found the situation as I related it in the first chapter.

The small group fellowship meetings in communities and in homes had already started. In fact, they followed wherever the new light of God's love spread. Those who had "risen from the dead," as it were, naturally gravitated to one another.

Then perhaps someone said he had been in a meeting of Bible study, sharing and prayer, and they tried it. One thing is certain, that no one came around to "organize follow-up."

Teams were going out, invited or not, at their own expense, from Rwanda to Burundi and Tanganyika, from western and central Uganda to other provinces, and to Kenya and Sudan. Word came back of evidences of God's power at work in all these places.

In Kigezi, in 1945, the first of the memorable Kabale Conventions was held to celebrate ten years of new life since the Holy Spirit graciously began reviving His Church after the first evangelistic team came in 1935. The theme of the Convention, written large over the outdoor platform, was "Jesus Satisfies." Blasio had lived only a short time after he first came to Kabale, but others of that first team from Rwanda were there. Hundreds came long distances to the gathering, while thousands of local people came on foot. Mera and I were there with our first daughter, baby Peace. We were teaching at Kabale at the time and helped to entertain guests.

An educational missionary from Tanganyika, who was there, appealed for teachers to come to a struggling boys' school in central Tanganyika. That was a shaft in my heart. When I mentioned it to Mera, she could not take it at first, but later, after prayer, she accepted that we go as missionaries to this country, which is now called Tanzania. By the end of the year, we were commissioned by our brethren, together with the Erisa Wakabi family, to be their teacher-missionaries to central Tanganyika at Dodoma, an arid land both physically and spiritually.

We were assured by our brothers and sisters, who had had more experience, that in our struggle against the hostilities of the Enemy we would be empowered by the Holy Spirit, who would keep our eyes turned toward the Lord Jesus. They said that, in seeing Him, the weakest believer is able to cope with the shocks of life.

We had a clear sense of God's call and a full expectation that new life in Christ would quickly come to that part of

Tanganyika. So we survived the rigors of the bus trip, the deck passage on the Lake Victoria steamer, and the dirty third-class railway coaches, which were packed with rowdy soldiers returning from the war zones of Egypt and Burma.

We could still praise God together in the first days at Dodoma, even when the two families of us—Wakabis had four little ones, we had one and were expecting a second—were given one tiny house that had been a servant's quarters. It was empty of all furniture and food, but well supplied with ticks. We also coped with the tick fever and malaria that followed in a few days, and settled in to learn two new languages.

What finally upset us was finding that our eager sharing of our testimonies was not acceptable to the missionaries and church leaders there. We had come thinking that we were going to see the whole country come under the fire of the Spirit of God. Isn't that what had happened in Kigezi and in many other places we had heard of? But here the doors kept shutting in our faces. People said:

"No, we don't like that sort of thing in our churches."

"No, we don't think that kind of testimony is Scriptural. We don't want you to bring in some strange doctrine to disturb our people."

We were completely taken aback and confused. We began to resent it because we were sure we knew the right way to start. Naturally, then, we called those who had closed the doors to us "enemies of the blessing" and treated them like that.

That put us in the wrong place. We were no longer sitting low at Jesus' feet, receiving His grace. We were judges on a high pedestal, pointing fingers. And, of course, as soon as you become judgmental, you become as cold as ice. You can't judge and bless anyone at the same time.

As we became more and more spiritually dry, we were puzzled. What had God called us to? Only to teach geography and science and never to preach?

As we were praying, God said to us, "Ah, dear ones, you are suffering from the sins of success."

"What do you mean, Lord?"

"You came from an area where everything was easy: meetings were warm, people were being saved, many were rejoicing. Now you have to change. You were feeding on successes instead of feeding on Me. I want you to learn a new lesson."

"What is it, Lord?"

"Please learn patience that does not demand experiences. You will find Me alone as the One who can satisfy you, direct you, and make you love the unlovable."

So we repented. We did not repent of our testimony, but of our attitude—a kind of holier-than-thou spirit that was hard and critical. Then the Lord began to send us to the homes of the people we had resented, to apologize and to ask forgiveness. Some didn't make it easy for us, but we began to be happy again. It cleared the air of the poisonous gases.

Then the Lord set us free to show our love in little ways to our former "enemies." We began to act as simple people who love Jesus, and so we found God brought us all kinds of opportunities to speak for Him along the path and in our homes.

What happened? Nothing at first. It was a long time before anything like fire was discernible around Dodoma, but here and there one or two sparks lighted, both in the community and in the school. A few school boys began to be drawn to us and they would come to talk.

About that time, there was one special lesson our Father had prepared to teach us. Mera had gone to the mission hospital thirty miles away for the delivery of our third child. I was keeping the first two at home near the school, which was two miles out of Dodoma. One day, Lydia, the second little girl, a beautiful child, went into convulsions. I tied her on my back and carried her on my bicycle, pedaling as hard as I could down that dusty road to the hospital in town.

In a matter of a few hours Jesus had taken our little girl to Himself. It was a shock and I wondered if it would kill me, and my wife when she heard about it. In that hospital ward I was surrounded by Muslims, for the town was predominantly Muslim. As I stood by that bed, I uttered a desperate little prayer and the Holy Spirit, the Dove of Heaven, was there to answer. I had hardly finished the little cry of pain when Heaven opened.

I had been looking at my little girl who was gone, with the most empty feeling you can have, when unexpectedly the Comforter brought in the Lord Jesus. He was my Saviour, I knew that, but at that moment He brought Heaven down and my heart was filled. Heaven became so close that it was as if the child had not died. I turned around and told the Muslims there about it and some of them wept in the hospital.

Then I prayed that my wife would experience the same, and I sent a messenger, with some trembling. I knew how she loved the little girl and I couldn't see how she could cope.

Mera loves Jesus, and the Comforter went immediately, before the runner got there. Our daughter, whom we named Joy, had been born the same day that Lydia died. And the Holy Spirit had come to the bed of this mother. When the message came, the unexpected took place. What my wife could never have done, she did. She got up and praised the Lord, and even told the other patients. Some have never forgotten that, especially those who knew our Lydia.

For a mother to go through that with a heart comforted and released was beyond their ability to understand. But she was able. God blessed her soul, and Heaven came near her, too.

When I went to fetch her in a friend's car, I had not seen her so free in the Lord. It was as if the Holy Spirit had taken the death of our child and turned it into a blessing for us. So one day we stood in the cathedral and sang the song "Loved with Everlasting Love," and our hearts were overflowing.

Other lessons we also had to learn, some of which were simply embarrassing.

Later that year we had reached the point where some of the high school boys were coming to our home once a week for Bible studies. They were keen to learn and I knew they looked up to me as their teacher.

One day after I came home from teaching, Mera and I had

a misunderstanding about something, and I went quiet. A fog settled between us. I had nothing to say, but the silence was hypocritical. Inside I was saying a lot and of course God knew it. I had forgotten the Bible Study group, when I heard the voices of the boys coming up the path to our house.

"Lord," I cried, "what shall I do? They're arriving and I have nothing to say to them. I'm in a mess. Help!"

Quietly the Lord said, "Don't try to give them a message. Just tell them who you are. It is time for them to find you in a mess. They will know you better."

I didn't like it at all, but there was nothing else for me to do. In the telling, I repented and God forgave me. When Mera came in, I asked her in front of them to forgive me too.

For the boys that was a time of new insights, and from that day some of them began to learn to walk with Jesus. Because doors were open to us now, the boys went out with us on weekends, singing and giving their testimonies. It was powerful. Churches were growing and eventually the Holy Spirit spread the light of Jesus all over central Tanzania.

We came to Dodoma expecting to stay three years, but we stayed eleven. During that time William Nagenda and Yosiya Kinuka had gone on preaching missions to England and Europe. With Dr. Church, William had gone to Indonesia, America, Brazil, India, and other countries. Invitations kept coming and it was exciting to hear what God was doing as the simple testimony of the grace of the Lord Jesus was shared in many countries.

In 1958 I was invited to accompany my dear brother, Tanzania's first African bishop, Yohana Omari, to Australia on a study and preaching tour. God greatly used Bishop Omari with his simple English and deep walk with the Lord.

During the months we were there, I was asked to travel north to preach to the Aborigines. The missionary explained in detail to me how unresponsive and hard to reach Aborigines always are. So I went to them with a built-in judgment.

True enough. When I spoke to them, I might as well have been speaking to stones: not a spark, not a glimmer of interest in anyone's eye. I began to wonder why I had come, and said to the missionary, "I think we made a mistake in coming here." But I had hardly finished my comment before the Spirit began to convict me.

"The problem is not with the Aborigines," He said. "It is with you. You had already made up your mind about them when you got here. You did not pour out your heart to them. You were speaking to yourself, so of course they could not hear."

I knelt down and asked forgiveness for my cold attitude. The Lord said, "All right. You just speak to them as My precious people for whom I died and forget everything you heard about them."

We had a small group of about twenty that evening, and I don't know what happened. I couldn't stop, and they responded. I saw one girl with tears streaming down her face. From then on it was quite different, and God did a work.

When we returned to Uganda, I enjoyed two years as a supervisor of schools. But the call to evangelism was strong and was affirmed now by many brothers and sisters. So Mera and I, with our four little girls, stepped out in faith, with no visible support, saying, "Yes, Lord, wherever You lead us."

Our Lord has been wonderfully faithful and has kept right on in His business of teaching us to walk humbly with Him through frequent traveling, through study and ordination, through starting the African Evangelistic Enterprise team, and through my being consecrated as Bishop of Kigezi.

At one time William Nagenda and I were sharing an exhausting preaching itinerary overseas. Along the way I became jealous of the success of my brother. I became critical of everything he said. Each sentence was wrong or ungrammatical or unscriptural. His gestures were hypocritical. Everything about my brother was wrong, wrong, wrong. The more I criticized, the colder I became. I was icy and lonely and homesick.

Then the Holy Spirit intervened. I didn't invite Him, but He has a lovely way of coming anyhow. He said quietly, "Festo, you are suffering."

"No, no. It is his fault." I had worked out carefully how to defend my case and expose my brother.

But He turned the whole thing around, saying, "*You* are not right! Whatever you see in your brother, your attitude is dry—dry as a bone. You are pushing him away."

Finally, I had to admit it. "No, Sir, I am not right. What shall I do?"

"There is nothing you can do about it. You are spiritually bankrupt at the moment. You had better make an application to Headquarters."

I turned to my Father in shame, confessing that my miserable attitude had affected my brother. For whenever you are cold toward another, you are stepping into the realm of murder.

Cain was asked, "Where is your brother?" and his answer, "I don't know," was a sign of murder.[1]

But when I admitted my sin, the cross instantly did its work. Jesus' blood cleansed me of it. I was free.

Then He said, "Go tell your brother why things were so cold."

I argued, "Lord, haven't I reached the stage now where You and I can finish things between us without this childish apologizing?" I knew He understood things quickly, but I wasn't sure how William would take it. Anyway, I had to go. He said so.

We were about to start off for a meeting where we were supposed to preach together, and I said, "William, I am sorry. I'm very sorry. You sensed the coldness."

"Yes, I felt the coldness, but I didn't know what had happened. What is it?"

"I became jealous of you. Please forgive me."

That dear brother got up and hugged me and we both shed tears of reconciliation. My heart was warm, and when he preached, the message spoke to me deeply. One thing he said was, "St. Paul didn't think that to admit failure was a blot on the gospel." He had read Paul's great words of praise: "Thanks be to God, who in Christ always leads us in triumph, and through us spreads the fragrance of the knowledge of him everywhere.''[2] Then he pointed out that just before that word of praise are the verses about his defeat in Troas: ''My spirit was restless when I came to Troas because I didn't find my brother Titus there, so even though a tremendous door was open and people were waiting to hear the gospel, I left them and came to Macedonia.''[3]

Wasn't Paul saying, ''I failed. I really went all to pieces in my disappointment . . . but thanks be to God for His grace which received me back and gave me *His* triumph, which is all His.'' When we are taken into the triumphal procession of the crucified, risen Christ, we are not saying we are perfect. What we do say is, ''Hallelujah! I am weak and sometimes fail, but thank God, He has made a perfect provision for me. The perfume is *His grace*.''

The lesson was a good one to learn. Were it not for His mercy, we would have fallen by the way long ago.

- - - - - -

[1] Genesis 4:9.
[2] 2 Corinthians 2:14, *RSV*.
[3] Personal paraphrase of 2 Corinthians 2:12,13.

CHAPTER 9

Love Triumphs in Suffering

Ever since the 1950's our brethren in one part or another of East Africa have been caught up in political turmoil in which they had no part, but under which they have suffered. In the midst of this, Calvary love has taught us all some important lessons.

First, in Kenya in the 1950's, the Mau Mau uprising aimed at turning the whole Kikuyu tribe into freedom fighters, using guerrilla tactics against the governing British. Although our Christian brethren agreed with the goal of national freedom, there was nothing on earth that would make them take the oath to murder that was demanded of them.

So hundreds of them were killed. They were attacked because the unity of the tribe, through oathing, was the first objective of the Mau Mau leaders. Christian resisters were quietly strangled on the path or chopped up with machetes at night in their homes.

Government officers, assuming that these suffering brethren must be their allies, offered them guns for self-protection. The answer was, ''No, thank you. We love you and we love our Kikuyu brothers as well. How can we tell the ones in the forest about the love of God if we are holding guns?'' And testify they did, as they died.

A few years later we heard about it from once-tough Mau Mau fighters who had turned to Christ. I remember one who stood up in a Kenya convention we held in 1958. Before eleven thousand people, he said, ''I was one who led a group of fighters to attack a Christian family at night. We were ordered to

73

do it because they were 'hard-core resisters.' But to my surprise, that man loved us. He said that he was not at all afraid to die, for he would immediately be with Jesus. Then he pleaded with us, not for *his* life, but for ours, that we awake and repent while there was still time. We killed him, but he died praying, 'Father, please forgive them and give them time to turn about.' We went back to the forest, but the face of that man and his love never left me. At last His Jesus has found me, and now I want to tell everyone about Him.'' This man became an evangelist and I have preached by his side.

How do you destroy Christians like that? You beat them; they love you. You put them to shame; they think you have given them an opportunity to be creative. You kill them and they win you!

The early disciples of Jesus were like that after the enthronement of the risen Christ in their hearts at Pentecost. When they were beaten terribly by the Sanhedrin, ''they left the Council chamber rejoicing that God had counted them worthy to suffer dishonor for his name.''[1] Paul and Silas were like that. In Philippi they were stripped and beaten with whips. With bleeding backs, feet clamped into stocks, they were praying and singing praises to the Lord at midnight and all the other prisoners were listening![2]

During the Mau Mau upheaval, a young schoolmaster named Heshbon was attacked in his office at the school. All the pupils ran for their lives. Heshbon's front teeth were knocked out and he was left for dead on the floor. God's people found him, tenderly nursed him, and he survived.

After two weeks, he insisted on going back to the same school, though he was offered another. He was possessed by the desire to find the men who attacked him and tell them that Jesus loves them. He thought that some of them might have been captured and put into a maximum security prison. So Heshbon went there, Bible in hand. He said to the British officer in charge, ''May I have permission to go in?''

''What for?''

''I want to tell your prisoners that Jesus loves them.''

"Are you mad? They would tear you limb from limb."

"Do you know who they are?" asked Heshbon gently.

"Yes, they are the toughest terrorists in the world."

"No, they are precious men for whom Christ died. I know them well, they are my brothers. Look at my mouth where the teeth are gone and at the scars on my face. They did it, so I want to tell them that Jesus died for them."

The officer was taken aback and finally said, "All right. In you go, but remember, it is at your own risk."

Heshbon stepped inside the walls. The prisoners were breathing like lions and came forward menacingly. He spoke to them in their mother tongue and opened his Bible, which they hated. But for thirty minutes they listened. When he finally came out, he left a number of the prisoners converted inside. The British officer said, "So you've come back, have you?"

"Yes, I'm all right, and I have left a few more like me in there."

There is a sort of invincibility—whether in death or life—about God's people who are living in the power of Calvary by the presence of the Holy Spirit. Because of what Jesus did on the cross, a new power has penetrated humanity. It is a new way of looking at men and things.

Both the countries of Rwanda and Burundi erupted into intertribal wars and massacres in the 1960's. I remember one of my brothers in Christ in Burundi, who stood before a group of soldiers who were about to execute him simply because he was one of the tribe hated by the government in power. I knew him personally.

He said to the gunmen, "Before you kill me, may I have permission to say a few things?"

"Say it quickly."

"First," he said, "I love you. Second, I love my country. Third, I will sing a song." In their mother tongue he sang all four verses of the hymn which starts:

> Out of my bondage, sorrow and night,
> Jesus, I come! Jesus, I come!

When he finished, they shot him. But he has not died, he

is still speaking. One of the messages which is being passed on from country to country is: "Death is not defeat. It is a glorious arrival, and we are all on the path toward the same Glory." Another message is: "Our only weapon is love."

In Uganda, during the eight years in the 1970's when Idi Amin and his men slaughtered probably half a million Ugandans, "We live today and are gone tomorrow" was the common phrase.

We learned that living in danger, when the Lord Jesus is the focus of your life, can be liberating. For one thing, you are no longer imprisoned by your own security, because there is none. So the important security that people sought was to be anchored in God.

As we testified to the safe place we had in Jesus, many people who had been pagan, or were on the fringes of Christianity, flocked to the church or to individuals, asking earnestly, "How do you prepare yourself for death?" Churches all over the country were packed both with members and seekers. This was no comfort to President Amin, who was making wild promises to Libya and other Arab nations that Uganda would soon be a Muslim country. (It is actually about 80 per cent Christian.)

Under persecution, there were frequent quiet meetings in homes, unobserved. We were asking the Lord to show us, in the situation that was upon us, how we could demonstrate His glory—His radiant character.

As we meditated, it became clear to us that the Church was born out of the sufferings of our Lord Jesus Christ. The reason He suffered was because He came as the Truth and the Light into a world of falsehood and darkness. Representatives of this darkness and untruth, hating His Light and Truth, attacked Him and in the end crucified Him. We, therefore, who have been born of Him are always liable to persecution, as He Himself told us, saying, "Where I am, there shall also my servant be."[3] This may be on a cross. He said, "The world will make you suffer. But take courage! I have defeated the world."[4]

When we stand where our Lord stood in this world, representing His Light and Truth, we are an embarrassment and a threat to darkness. We are likely to be hated and called "a subversive community." This happened to us in Uganda.

It became clear to us through the Scriptures that our resistance was to be that of overcoming evil with good.[5] This included refusing to cooperate with anything that dehumanizes people, but we reaffirmed that we can never be involved in using force or weapons.

Therefore we knew, of course, that the accusation against our beloved brother, Archbishop Janani Luwum, that he was hiding weapons for an armed rebellion, was untrue, a frame-up to justify his murder.

The archbishop's arrest, and the news of his death, was a blow from the Enemy calculated to send us reeling. That was on February 16, 1977. The truth of the matter is that it boomeranged on Idi Amin himself. Through it he lost respect in the world and, as we see it now, it was the beginning of the end for him.

For us, the effect can best be expressed in the words of the little lady who came to arrange flowers, as she walked through the cathedral with several despondent bishops who were preparing for Archbishop Luwum's Memorial Service. She said, "This is going to put us twenty times forward, isn't it?" And as a matter of fact, it did.

More than four thousand people walked, unintimidated, past Idi Amin's guards to pack St. Paul's Cathedral in Kampala on February 20. They repeatedly sang the "Martyrs' Song," which had been sung by the young Ugandan martyrs in 1885. Those young lads had only recently come to know the Lord, but they loved Him so much that they could refuse the evil thing demanded of them by King Mwanga. They died in the flames singing, "Oh that I had wings such as angels have, I would fly away and be with the Lord." They were given wings, and the singing of those thousands at the Memorial Service had wings too.

We have no way of estimating the fresh impetus given by

the martyrdom of Luwum to the Body of Christ. In Heaven we will know. After the service in the cathedral, the crowd gathered outside around the little cemetery where a grave had been dug for Janani beside that of Bishop Hannington, the first bishop for Central Africa sent out from England to the young church in Uganda. He was martyred by the same king in the same year as the boys.

Our archbishop's grave was empty because we had been denied the body of our leader. Soldiers had taken it far north to his own village of Kitgum for burial, in order to avoid the embarrassment to Amin of the discovery that he had died by bullets, not by a car accident as was pretended. At the open grave, former Archbishop Erica Sabiti quoted the words of the angels at the empty tomb of Jesus, "He is not here, He is risen!" Instantly a song of Zion burst out with such power that "Glory, glory, hallelujah" was heard from that hilltop far into the city.

Jesus' death on the cross was a climax of victory, not of defeat. His resurrection was the proof and seal of this victory. To the world, a martyr's death may seem like a tragedy, but we saw our archbishop as a witness in whose life the cross was reenacted. Our youngest daughter was at this Memorial Service and reported it to us. Mera and I were not there.

We had returned to our home in Kabale on Saturday at the urgent request of many in Kampala. Several high-level persons had reported that I was now at the head of Amin's death list.

When we reached home, we were told that Amin's men had been there three times that day looking for me. Our brothers and sisters would not even let us pack or unpack anything, but urged us to flee as we were across the border that night. "One bishop's death this week is enough for us," they said.

God was certainly with them as they took over to organize our escape. A young couple, who are dear to us, left their five little children at home to drive us in their Land Rover by a back road to the mountains on the border. We got lost in the dark. For hours we wandered along a footpath which skirted a deep lake. Several times we nearly tumbled into the lake, but the time was not lost, for when we managed to return to the main road, the roadblock at the bridge had been taken away for the night.

When we reached a mountain village, which was as far as a vehicle could go, some people who were quietly awakened took care of everything: a guide for the mountain trail and help with our bags. God gave Mera strength to keep climbing slowly, though she had a fever from bronchitis and was wearing a long skirt which dragged in the mud. We learned later that none of our helpers was discovered by the secret service agents after it became known that we had escaped. God kept them secret!

At dawn on the Sunday morning of Luwum's Memorial, we were having a little praise service, sitting on a big rock just across the border in Rwanda. As the sun came up, we remembered that verse: "Unto you that fear my name shall the Sun of righteousness arise with healing in his wings."[6] How we prayed for that righteousness and healing in our dear homeland out of which we had escaped.

A suffering Church can bless a nation and provide a refuge to which the suffering society may turn for healing, for liberation and hope. This was proved in Uganda as the Church came under more systematic attack, and hundreds of martyrs' deaths were added to that of the archbishop's. Those of us in exile also were able to be of some help to the thousands of refugees pouring out of Uganda with only the clothes on their backs. Some doctors fled straight from their hospitals, one in the midst of surgery he couldn't finish. My daughter was one of hundreds who had to flee from Makerere University, and she had to run in the middle of her final exams.

Later some of those who were helped to find work or scholarships in colleges said that the one place where they found love and were restored to human dignity was at our little African Evangelistic Enterprise office in Nairobi. All of us had the melting experience of discovering brothers and sisters around the world who prayed for us, then opened their arms and their purse strings to receive and comfort the destitute. We have had a revelation of God's worldwide family.

One deep lesson many of us struggled with has been to forgive the unforgivable. Many have argued with me about the title of my little book, "*I Love Idi Amin*."[7] And I can only go back to that first Good Friday after our escape from Uganda. We were in England and the newspapers were reporting daily the increased persecution back home. The six young actors who were to have represented the early martyrs of Uganda in a play for the church's Centennial Celebration were found dead together in a field. And on and on.

With the pain we had already gone through, I felt something was strangling me spiritually. I grew increasingly bitter toward Amin, and was, to the same degree, losing my liberty and my ministry.

I slipped into the back of All Souls Church in London to listen to the meditations on the seven last words of Christ on the cross.

The first word was read distinctly: "Father, forgive them; for they do not know what they are doing."[8] So said my Lord when the cruel nails were being driven into His hands. His amazing love pressed into my consciousness. To me He was saying, "You can't forgive Amin?"

"No, Lord."

"Suppose he had been one of those soldiers driving the nails into My hands. He could have been, you know."

"Yes, Lord, he could."

"Do you think I would have prayed, 'Father, forgive them, all except that Idi Amin'?"

I shook my head. "No, Master. Even he would have come within the embrace of Your boundless love." I bowed, asking forgiveness. And, although I frequently had to repent and pray again for forgiveness, I rose that day with a liberated heart and have been able to share Calvary love in freedom. Yes, because of His immeasurable grace to me, I do love Idi Amin, have forgiven him, and am still praying for him to escape the terrible spiritual prison he is in.

Those who have experienced the reality of it proclaim confidently our Lord's promise to St. Paul, "My grace *is* enough for you: for where there is weakness, my power is shown the more completely."[9] Yes, God's power is demonstrated when His people are weak. Each one of His witnessing community is only a fragile vessel of clay, so that the great power is of God, not of ourselves. People will forget who bore witness, they will only remember what Jesus said and will reply with St. Paul, "I can even enjoy weaknesses, suffering, privations, persecutions and difficulties for Christ's sake. For my weakness makes me strong in him."[10]

God's messengers are not protected from "the slings and arrows of outrageous fortune," as the Greek cults believed of their semi-divine heroes. Instead, the exposure of weak, human vessels to all the opposing forces which are intent on destroying them may demonstrate the triumph of God's grace and power, just as the cross of Christ did. The purpose of this exposure is the release of life for others. We do not lose heart, knowing that "the grace which is spreading to more and more people may cause the giving of thanks to abound to the glory of God."[11]

In Uganda the Amin persecution never closed the churches. They continued crowded. People marched in great numbers at the celebration of the Centenary of the Church of Uganda, wearing the special clothes they had prepared. But, in talking it over, we agreed that even if all the churches had been closed, the life of the Body of Christ would have gone right on in the love-fellowship meetings in secret and in the predawn home worship that kept our eyes focused on the Lord Jesus and our hearts bowed before His cross. Nothing short of the power of His resurrection in the center of our lives makes it possible to meet the onslaughts of the Enemy.

Jesus took the Devil seriously throughout His life. Many times He brought to light the works of evil and routed them. He aroused all the antagonism of the Adversary and in the end defeated him on behalf of His people. For on the cross Jesus met the full force of the Enemy intent on destroying Him, and He overcame him publicly. This fact is well known in the spiritual realm. Calvary was a victory of love. Jesus shed no blood but His own. He overcame evil with good. Love was, and is now, triumphant.

That is why we shall stand one day together before that Great Throne in Heaven with the multitude that no one can number, out of every tribe and people and tongue and nation.

Before whom shall we be standing? Before the Throne of the *Lamb*.

And what will be our song to Him? "Worthy is the Lamb who was slain to receive power, and riches, and wisdom, and strength, and honor, and glory, and blessing."[12]

And the heavenly interpreter will explain: "These are the ones who come out of the great tribulation, and washed their robes and made them white in the blood of the Lamb."[13]

Hallelujah!

- - - - - -

[1] Acts 5:41, *LB*.
[2] Acts 16:22-25.
[3] John 12:26, *KJV*.
[4] John 16:33, *TEV*.
[5] Romans 12:21.
[6] Malachi 4:2, *KJV*.
[7] Fleming Revell, Old Tappan, NJ, 1977.
[8] Luke 23:34, *NASV*.
[9] 2 Corinthians 12:9, *Phillips*.
[10] 2 Corinthians 12:10, *Phillips*.
[11] 2 Corinthians 4:15, *NASV*.
[12] Adapted from Revelation 7:9 and 5:12.
[13] Revelation 7:14, *NKJV*.

A word about...
AFRICAN ENTERPRISE

African Enterprise is a group of men and women from many different denominations, races, tribes and nations. What binds them together in ministry is their deep love of Jesus Christ and their desire to help make Him known to others.

They seek primarily to be servants of the Church in Africa. Their five Africa-based teams respond to the invitation of local African churches and groups of churches to assist them in evangelism, and—in that context—to also help them meet emergency human needs.

By channeling this entire Christian ministry through the local church, Africans can minister to their fellow Africans in the name of our Lord. This means that African Enterprise—while incurring only minimal administrative costs—can significantly touch the lives of thousands of men, women and children throughout more than thirty countries of Africa.

African Enterprise was founded in 1962 by Michael Cassidy, a native South African, while he was a seminary student in the United States. Today he leads the two A.E. teams based in South Africa and Zimbabwe.

In 1970, Festo Kivengere, an East African evangelist whose spiritual impact was already worldwide, founded the three African Enterprise teams in Uganda, Kenya and Tanzania.

Today the ministry is by no means limited to Africa. Teams share with increasing numbers of receptive audiences around the world the good news of God's love and the exciting work of Christ today in Africa.

And wherever they minister, reconciliation takes place. In the power of the Spirit, men and women become reconciled to God...and then become reconciled to one another as they discover together their oneness in Jesus Christ.

African Enterprise is governed by an International Council of delegates from ten countries around the world.

I Dared to Call Him Father

by Bilquis Sheikh
with Richard Schneider

This is a book for everyone who wonders what would happen if he gave himself to God completely. 'Will he really fulfil his promises to take care of me — to protect me under all conditions?'

It is the true story of Bilquis Sheikh, a Pakistani woman of noble birth who faced such questions at the crossroads of her life. After she was left by her husband (a high-ranking government official), she retreated to her family estate to find peace and live out her days in quiet luxury. But the deep-down peace she sought eluded her. Searching in the Koran, she found many references to the prophet Jesus. Out of curiosity, she turned to the pages of the Christian Bible.

Then her life turned upside down as a series of strange dreams launched her on a quest that would consume her heart, mind and soul.

Kingsway Publications

The Cross Behind Bars

The true story of Noel Proctor—
Prison Chaplain

by Jenny Cooke

As a boy, Noel Proctor thought that God didn't live outside the Sunday School classroom. Until something happened that was to turn his life upside down and launch him into a totally unexpected career: chaplain to one of Her Majesty's prisons.

Noel soon discovered that he couldn't convert the hardened inmates of Britain's prisons singlehanded. God had to do a deeper work in his life before revival could come to the nation's 'forgotten people'.

This is the warm and intimate account of how one man learned to live in the power and will of God, and how his wife found the courage to fight 'terminal' cancer. Above all it shows how God's power can be released when his people put him first in their lives.

Noel Proctor *held chaplaincies at Wandsworth, Eastchurch and Dartmoor Prisons before becoming Senior Chaplain at Strangeways in Manchester.*

Jenny Cooke *is an adult education tutor who teaches creative writing. She is married with three children.*

Kingsway Publications